C.2

Writing Screenplays
by
Jessie Coleman
and Paul Peditto

D0465421

Self-Counsel Press
(a division of)
International Self-Counsel Press Ltd.
USA   Canada

Self-Counsel Press acknowledges the financial support of the Government of Canada through the Canada Book Fund (CBF) for our publishing activities.

Printed in Canada.

First edition: 2012

Library and Archives Canada Cataloguing in Publication

Coleman, Jessie

  Writing screenplays / Jessie Jamie Coleman, Paul Peditto.

Includes index.
ISBN 978-1-77040-104-4

1. Motion picture authorship. I. Peditto, Paul II. Title.

PN1996.C65 2012   808.2'3   C2011-907044-8

Self-Counsel Press
(a division of)
International Self-Counsel Press Ltd.

| Bellingham, WA | North Vancouver, BC |
| USA | Canada |

contents

Appendix   89

Resources   183

Worksheets

Samples

Notice to Readers

Laws are constantly changing. Every effort is made to keep this publication as current as possible. However, the author, the publisher, and the vendor of this book make no representations or warranties regarding the outcome or the use to which the information in this book is put and are not assuming any liability for any claims, losses, or damages arising out of the use of this book. The reader should not rely on the author or the publisher of this book for any professional advice. Please be sure that you have the most recent edition.

Dedication & Acknowledgments

Since no one in this business accomplishes anything without the help of others, I would be remiss to not give credit where credit is due.

Love and kisses to my wonderful family and friends, especially McCoy and Lennon who have encouraged my literary endeavors over the years. Many thanks and much appreciation to managing editor Eileen Velthuis, who believed in this project from the very beginning. And finally, I want to thank my editor Tanya Lee Howe for the fabulous work she did in shaping our book into something I can be proud of.

— Jessie Jamie Coleman

This book is dedicated to my father, who taught style, and Claire Gerardi, who was *Jane Doe*, and who won't be forgotten.

— Paul Peditto

Introduction

Everyone has a story to tell. Never before have personal narratives gushed so profusely in North America as they do this present day. It seems everyone wants to tell his or her life story. Is it because we believe our lives are all unique, or is it that we think people can learn from our drama? Is it a combination of both? Regardless of the reasons writers have for wanting to tell their life stories, as long as people exist, there will never be a shortage of people wanting to put forth their life woes or adventures.

Do you think your life would make a good movie? Most people do, and the reason is simple: There is a story to tell in all of us.

The truth of the matter is, everyone *does* have a story worth telling, if he or she knows how to do it. That's what this book is about — helping writers find that crossroad, locate that milestone, and hone in on that moment in time that has lessons for everyone. However, just because something has happened to you doesn't necessarily mean it will make a good movie, but there *are* moments in everyone's life that, with the right spin, could make for a dramatic work of art.

It's also true that there are many books on the market regarding the subjects of screenplays and memoir writing; however, *Writing Screenplays* dares to be different. This pioneering how-to guide walks the reader through a step-by-step process of telling the true-life tale in screenplay format, which is uniquely different from the standard book format. The screenplay version of your life story will cut to the meat of your story and highlight the message you want to share. You could say this book is two books in one:

- It's a book about honing in on your life's most dramatic moments and fleshing out the story into something people would want to know.

- It's a book about how to craft a story made for the screen (whether TV or the big screen).

It is our wish that you enjoy the adventures of *Writing Screenplays* and, at the very least, experience the wonderful and fun process of discovery by connecting with the moments in your life that made you the person you are today. Here's a golden opportunity to share with the world the story that is unique to you and demands to be told.

The following are some of our favorite movies based on true stories:

Jessie's picks:

- *Antwone Fisher*
- *The Assassination of Richard Nixon*
- *Black Hawk Down*
- *Deliberate Intent*
- *Introducing Dorothy Dandridge*

- *Men of Honor*
- *Mississippi Burning*
- *Not Without My Daughter*
- *The People vs. Larry Flynt*
- *Seabiscuit*

Paul's picks:

- *Bobby*
- *Capote*
- *Donnie Brasco*
- *Factory Girl*
- *GoodFellas*

- *Marie Antoinette*
- *Primary Colors*
- *Sylvia*
- *United 93*
- *W.*

The Appendix contains coauthor Paul Peditto's screenplay *Pictures of Baby Jane Doe*. It is a graphic story, based on a real person he knew. Real life is graphic so it was important to include this screenplay as an example.

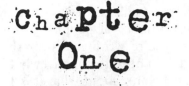

Chapter One

Finding Your Story

Your mission, if you should choose to accept it, is to select the most interesting period of your life that will appeal to a large audience. Your movie can be a drama, comedy, romance, etc., but if you want the movie to sell, you need to be aware of what the marketplace is buying. If you want your script to appeal to a movie audience, it must resonate with them; it must ring true with a theme that is universal, with characters the audience can recognize as believable and real.

True-life stories continue to cast a spell over people who want to learn from the experience of others, and for that reason, true-life stories with universal appeal will always be in high demand. For example, an adaptation that was powerful and had universal appeal was *The Fighter*, about the real-life battles of "Irish" Micky Ward and his rise to a boxing championship despite his dysfunctional family.

There are always moments or dramatic events in our lives that are so fascinating or memorable that they scream to be shared with the world, and we think, "This could be a movie!" Though that may very well be true, how do you go about finding that moment in time worth writing about and sharing with the world?

You may feel that the challenge is to choose the story that would appeal to the largest number of people. You want to be aware of what will sell, but if you're writing this for the audience alone, it won't be much good. You need to channel what I believe Judith Malina once said, "First I think about what it is I want to say. Then I go about saying it." The point is that the story you're writing must resonate with you; it's a story that you *need* to write, not one that will draw the largest number of people.

Remember, a story is not necessarily interesting because it really happened. It's an interesting story simply because it is, whether it really happened or not. Think of your life story as a work of fiction. If your life story were pitched as a novel, would people line up to purchase a copy, or would you have to say, "based on a true story" to capture their attention? You want your life story to be so interesting that even if it were not a true story, it would be compelling all on its own.

While you are in the planning stages of your story, it might be a good idea to view a few true-life stories on film to get an idea of how the subject matter is handled. After you have viewed some movies, you will probably have a better sense of how different stories are executed based on theme. If you have already decided upon the story you wish to tell, congratulations! If not, I offer you a piece of advice: Look for the hot spots of your life, the moments of the greatest change, greatest lessons, and sometimes the greatest loss. Do this and you will find the story that only you can tell. Here's a golden opportunity to share with the world the story that is unique to you and demands to be told.

1. Story Ideas to Get You Started

Where is the story in your life? What part of your life should be shared with the world? Instead of looking for just that *one* story to tell, compile a list of several stories from which to choose. The key is to tap into your own personal stories, and find something universal that will resonate with total strangers.

The following sections will help you get started compiling your list of story ideas. Of course, this list is in no way conclusive. You will probably find many other wonderful points of interest.

1.1 School days

It doesn't matter whether it was grade school, high school, college, grad school, medical school, or law school; if you dig up enough dirt, you will find something hidden in the shadows worth discussing. Ask yourself the following questions:

- What happened to you during your school days?
- Were you bullied until you learned to defend yourself?
- Did you pursue a major for the sake of pleasing your parents?
- Were you partying so much that you ended up cheating just to get passing grades?

Movies such as *Fast Times at Ridgemont High*, *Mean Girls*, and *Heathers* aren't based on true stories, but they are all about the trials and tribulations of high school. If you want to write about your school days, watch movies (nonfiction and fiction) to get an idea of what the audience wants in a school-based movie.

1.2 Children

You may want to write stories for kids about adventures you and your friends had, or you may want to write about your children and the struggles you have had with them.

- Were you blessed with a baby when the doctor told you that you only had a 10 percent chance of conceiving?
- Did you want a girl, but ended up with a boy and realized it was a boy you really wanted all along?
- Did you try for a baby for years, then stop trying only to become pregnant the next month?
- Did you and your childhood friends have a great adventure? (Even though *Stand by Me* isn't a true story, it is a good reference for a group of kids bonding while searching for adventure.)

You may want to write about a darker time in your teenage years. A good movie to watch is *Thirteen*. Nikki Reed co-wrote and co-starred in the movie. Reed was a teenager at the time of writing.

1.3 Animals

Stories about animals can be funny or inspiring. If you are an animal lover, maybe this is a topic at which you can excel.

- Do you love your pet so much that you are single because you always put your pet first?

- Did you lose your pet and swore you would never adopt another one?

- Do you have funny or inspiring stories about your pets?

- Did you ever work in a pet shop or veterinarian clinic and have funny stories to share about the customers and their animals?

1.4 Family traditions, religious experiences, and vacations

Every family has their own holiday rituals. Some of them are hilarious. For example, does your family have a ritual of take-no-prisoners chess matches and Monopoly games during the holidays? Or maybe your family has a unique way of decorating the tree?

There are also religious traditions. Who doesn't have an insanely religious aunt or uncle who would make a great movie character?

- Did you fall in love with someone of a different race or background and have to flee the country just so you two could be together?

- How do you feel now about your family's passed-down traditions and beliefs? How will those traditions affect your children?

- Did you have a religious awakening after a traumatic life event?

- Are there family feuds that continue from year to year at family gatherings?

- Are you so religious that people find you to be a fanatic?

- Did you refuse to date someone you really liked because you and this person did not share the same religion?

- Did you attend an awkward funeral for an eccentric relative?

- Is your birthday one of your favorite or least favorite holidays?

- Which holiday is more significant to you? Valentine's Day or New Year's Eve? Has that changed over the years?

Pieces of April is a fabulous movie about a daughter attempting to prepare a Thanksgiving dinner for her estranged family. Another example is *A Christmas Story*, which is a movie classic, from the memories of Jean Shepherd (based on the book of short stories *In God We Trust, All Others Pay Cash*).

People love memorable vacation movies. Take the time to watch box-office hits such as *Home Alone* and any of the National Lampoon's *Vacation* movies. These movies may be fictional, but audiences loved them!

- Do you have any funny vacation stories that you can share with the world?

- Was there ever a particular vacation that brought you so much pain that you wished you could have skipped it?

- Did you have a vacation that did not go as planned where one bad thing happened after another?

1.5 Siblings

Sibling stories can be funny or serious and may include stories about sibling rivalries, or adapting to living with step or adopted siblings. In serious drama, conflict between siblings can be fatal (e.g., Michael and Fredo Corleone in *The Godfather*).

- When you were growing up, did you cherish your baby sister or brother?

- Did you have a love for your older brother that other people found unusual (e.g., consider Angelina Jolie and the media frenzy that occurred around her relationship with her brother, James Haven)?

- Did you model your behavior after your older sister because you thought the world of her? What's the relationship like now? Is it the same or different?

- Did you wish you were an only child because your sibling received all of your parents' attention?

- Did your sister or brother pick on you and blame you for everything? Or did your parents automatically blame you for something your brother or sister did?

- Are you still close with your siblings, or are you still on non-speaking terms?

There is a discussion about sibling rivalries in movies at www.aceshowbiz.com/news/view/00017186.html.

1.6 Love and heartbreak

There are numerous stories about love and heartbreak. The key is to understand what moves you in life and whether or not your story will be moving for the audience. What could be more universal than writing about one of your great loves?

- Did you meet someone online? If so, did you lose all sense of reason when you found yourself engaged after only knowing each other for one month?

- Have you ever been so in love that you actually considered murdering someone?

- Would you have shaved ten years off your life to be with a certain person?

- Did you have a whirlwind romance that lasted for six months and then abruptly stopped?

- Were you so much in love and/or lust that you and your romantic interest barricaded yourselves inside a hotel room for one week?

- Were you so in love and/or lust that you couldn't think straight?

- Had you given up on love and then soon after met the love of your life?

- Did you disappear from your friends and family for a period of time because of your obsession with your new love interest?

- Do you still speak to the person you want to write about?

1.7 Employment

Employment stories can be entertaining (e.g., *Waiting* … , *Office Space*, *The Devil Wears Prada*, or *The Nanny Diaries*). Almost everybody has a job, and most people have had to endure a horrible boss or coworker, so the audience can relate to a good employment story.

- Did you hate your job so much that you quit even though you needed the money?

- Did you suffer a mental breakdown after the loss of a job?

- Was there a time in your life where your job was your only source of companionship?

- Did you ever have a job in which your coworker or boss sabotaged your career advancement?

1.8 Parents

Stories about parents can be serious, sad, or happy. From parents who were neglectful to parents who were overprotective, the possibilities under this topic are endless. A good reference is the dark comedy *Welcome to the Dollhouse*, which covers family relationships.

- Were you so close with your parents, you could tell them things other kids wouldn't dare share with their parents?

- Did the relationship with your parents make you want to be a parent?

- Did you hate your parents for the longest time until you became a parent yourself? If so, what's that relationship like now?

1.9 Dirty secrets

Who doesn't have dirty secrets? Do you dare write about your own dirty secrets?

- Did you harbor a secret that you would do anything to keep under wraps?

- Were you ruined by a secret that got out?

- Are you keeping a secret now?

1.10 Health and wellness

Health and wellness stories can cover a variety of topics such as mental illness or a physical disability and coping with the effects of the illness. *Running with Scissors* is a harrowing story of a son's difficult relationship with his mother and her questionable mental health.

- Did you have a health scare that made you see life in a totally new light?

- Were you diagnosed with an illness that changed your life?

- Were/are you a health nut because of something that happened to a friend or family member?

- What's your health situation now?

1.11 Undying aspirations

There are many stories that can be told about undying aspirations. For example, *The Positively True Adventures of the Alleged Texas Cheerleader-Murdering Mom* is based on the true story of a Texas mom who tries to hire a hit man to kill a cheerleader and/or the cheerleader's mother.

- Did you always want to be an actress but were afraid you would fail?

- Did you want to play sports professionally but were afraid your parents would not approve?

- Would you have done anything to be a dancer?

- How has not following your dreams affected your life?

- What dream would you like to pursue now?

1.12 Accomplishments and overcoming obstacles

Accomplishments and overcoming obstacles can range from getting over an addiction to getting hired at your dream job.

Lots of families have drug-addicted sons, daughters, mothers, and fathers. What do you do when tough love isn't enough? How about writing about it? This is how you get a movie made, by plumbing your own emotional depths to find a truth greater than yourself that will resonate with an audience. When people recognize their own relatives in your movie, your writing will truly move to another level. It's why the movie *The Fighter* was so powerful. Christian Bale's character is an addict, but his character's mother is in denial. The movie's journey is as much the story of Bale's character and his mother's acceptance of this addiction as it is the victory of Mark Wahlberg's character in the ring.

Another movie about addiction is coauthor Paul Peditto's *Pictures of Baby Jane Doe* (you will find the entire script in the Appendix). The story studies addiction from the point of view of the enabler.

You can tell your story from whatever angle you know best whether you were the addict, or someone you knew was the addict, and show how the addiction affected loved ones.

- Did you go from making $50,000 to $100,000 a year (or vice versa)?

- Were you at the top of your graduating class?

- Did you figure out an answer to a problem that stumped everyone else around you for months?

- Did you overcome an addiction when everyone else had given up on you?

- Are you living the life of your dreams? If not, ask yourself why?

If you want to see an inspiring true story, watch *127 Hours*. The story is based on the mountain climber, Aron Lee Ralston, who overcame incredible odds to survive.

1.13 Marriage and divorce

The topics of marriage and divorce can be serious or funny, you just have to remember to connect with your audience.

- Did you marry the wrong person?

- Was getting married the best or worst decision you ever made?

- Did marriage teach you something that you would like to share with others?

- What do you think about marriage now?

- Do you regret your divorce?

- Was getting a divorce the best or worst thing that could have ever happened to you? Did/will you marry again?

1.14 Life's crossroads

There are many crossroads in life. The key is to find the crossroad that had the most impact on your life and that will impact the most on your audience.

- Were you emotionally altered by a specific event?

- Was there a time when you thought you would not make it, but you did?

- Have you ever given up on life?

- Did someone say or do something to you that set you on a new life course? Where are you now because of that decision?

- Have you ever strived and struggled to accomplish something, then after not succeeding, realized it was not what you wanted all along?

2. Choosing the Right Moment for Your Story

Now that we have glossed over possible angles for your life story and the wheels are turning in your head, what's next? Choose one of the following:

- The moment in time where there was the most drama and pain. You may say, "but there were so many!" I know, I know. Just pick one.

- The moment in time that you find the most fascinating, whether good or bad fascination.

- The moment in time where you learned your biggest lesson.

- The moment in time that put you on a new course of life.

- The moment in time when you strived and struggled and then won.

Memoirs are about certain, unique, sometimes life-transforming periods as opposed to a whole life. You want to choose a story where somebody does something and something happens as a result, and how it affects the person negatively or positively in the end. The following are some examples:

- A woman graduates from medical school, then realizes that she really wanted to be a lawyer.

- A man searches for Mrs. Right for ten years only to learn that he really prefers to be with Mr. Right!

Now it's your turn to choose your moment in time to focus your story. You do this by forming a one- to two-sentence description (i.e., logline: very short description of concept, main character, and main conflict) similar to the above examples. Before you compile your description, I want to share with you the two different approaches you can take in weaving your true-life tale into an intimate dramatization.

2.1 Logline

When you have finished either Worksheet 1 or 2 (choose one), you will create your *logline* (i.e., a 25-word or less description of your movie). It sums up the whole movie in a sentence or two. Sounds difficult, but it's not. Every great logline has these three elements: who, goal, and obstacle. For example:

- When a Roman general is betrayed and his family murdered by an emperor's corrupt son, he comes to Rome as a gladiator to seek revenge. *Gladiator*

- A journey of self-discovery by a brilliant mathematician once he is diagnosed with schizophrenia. He eventually triumphs over tragedy and receives the Nobel Prize. *A Beautiful Mind*

- The aging patriarch of an organized crime dynasty transfers control of his clandestine empire to his reluctant son. *The Godfather*

Now it's time to craft your logline:

It's a story about a _____ who does _____ and _____ happens.

Play around with this description for a little while until you find something you feel really good about. This is the tough part. Once you get this description written down, the rest should be easy; then again, maybe not!

There are two sample loglines in Chapter 7.

WORKSHEET 1
Your Story: Approach 1

The first approach is to make your story a goal-oriented tale, in which the main character pursues some type of goal. An example would be a story about a person in search of a romantic partner. The middle of the story would focus on obstacles and problems throughout his or her journey, and the story would end when the main character accomplishes his or her goal (or not).

If you decide to take this approach, try to answer the following questions for the story you have in mind:

1. When does the event take place?

2. Who is/are the main character(s)?

3. Does/do the main character(s) have a goal to pursue?

4. Is the goal accomplished in the end?

5. Can you list the obstacles that the main character overcame on his or her journey?

6. Does/do your character(s) learn a lesson in the end, or does a change occur along the way? How?

7. Who is/are the secondary character(s)?

8. How are the secondary characters related to the main character(s)?

9. Do any of these secondary characters have goals of their own? If yes, what are they?

WORKSHEET 2
Your Story: Approach 2

The second approach is to make your story about "everything that happened on the way to the market." This is my favorite type of tale because it is usually a character-driven piece. An example of this type of story would be a person who takes a road trip with a friend, and the story is about everything that happened to them along the way.

If you're interested in this approach, try to answer the following questions for the story you have in mind:

1. When does this event take place?

2. How long does this event take (e.g., over a weekend, month, year, or summer)?

3. Who is/are the main character(s)?

4. What happens in the end?

5. Can you list everything that happened on the way to the end (e.g., on my way to Florida, my car was stolen, I twisted my ankle, and I caught a cold)?

6. Does/do the character(s) learn a lesson in the end, or does a change occur along the way?

7. Who are the secondary characters, and how do they relate to the main character(s)?

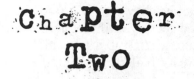

Chapter Two

Creating Memorable Characters

Strike a chord with people. Write something that resonates. Synthesize the personal into something that will read and view as universal. But how do you write characters that resonate, and who will mean something to the audience? In all "moviedom" there are only three types of character models:

1. Characters that exist in the real world.

2. Characters that are wholly invented.

3. Characters that are a combination of 1 and 2.

As the writer, you are God because you invent the characters and the world in which they live. You decide every breath every character in your movie will take. Characters based strictly on people you know in the real world can sometimes turn sentimental and lose perspective. Then again, if you base your characters entirely on fiction, they may be stiff and lack real-life passion, dialogue, or humor.

Oftentimes what happens in real life cannot be believed, let alone invented. Ever see anyone eat baby back ribs like your Uncle Rocky?

How about your pal Mickey who works the graveyard shift at the adult bookstore and feeds you dialogue no human being has ever uttered in your presence? Grab a pen and write down every word Mickey says because it's real life; use it all.

Someone at the post office looks exactly like the antagonist you imagined in your story? Record the physical details of the person, the way he or she moves, and what he or she says. Stranger than fiction, you usually cannot beat what the real world offers. If you hear someone say something, and it's good, record it on your computer or in a notebook. Assuming it's not a passage from someone else's published work, if you hear it and write it down, you just wrote it.

Character development will always take center stage in the process of creating compelling characters (whether fiction or nonfiction). Even though you will be writing about characters who already exist, your job as an effective screenwriter is to define who they are, what they want, and flesh them out into unforgettable characters that readers will want to read about and cheer for.

We all know that characters can make or break a story. If the audience does not care what happens to your characters, you don't really have a story, so what is the point of writing it? In saying that, before we talk about creating character backgrounds, let's first talk about what makes an intriguing character.

1. Creating Intriguing Characters

A great way to define an interesting character is to look at the characteristics that make us remember people in real life. Make a list of two types of characters: sympathetic and non-sympathetic. A story about a rich snob who goes from party to party bored with life with zero ambition, not knowing what to do with his life will probably *not* strike much sympathy with an audience.

Here are some of the characteristics that make a real-life person as well as a fictional character interesting:

- **Genuinely nice people:** People who say positive things about us and do nice things for us. This group might include people who are concerned about the welfare of others, forgiving people, and people who generally do the right and ethical thing. Basically, this is a group of people who make us feel good. Think about the people in your life you like the most. Do they make you feel good?

- **Smart and successful people:** People who are at the top of their field and who have achieved great success.

- **Eccentric, funny, or bold people:** People who are not afraid to be original even if it means making a fool of themselves; people who make us laugh or smile.

Examples of characters who are interesting include Jane Eyre, who was beaten down; Amélie, who always thought about others first; and the characters in *3:10 to Yuma* who bury their dead and move their wagons west. Speaking of Westerns, how about the classic Clint Eastwood character in *Unforgiven*, one of the greatest westerns of all time? This character is neither likeable nor sympathetic, yet we can't take our eyes off of him. Note that obsession and revenge will never go out of style!

After you have cast your story, analyze each principal character to see if any of them can pass the "interesting" test. Please note that it is not necessary that all your principal characters be likeable or interesting. Some characters are meant to be the exact opposite and that is fine, just as long as it's not your main character who's not interesting. Having one interesting character is fine, but more than one is even better.

Some of the greatest movie characters are not likeable. What you want are characters who are truthful, poignant, and compelling. Memorable characters such as Dr. Hannibal Lecter (*The Silence of the Lambs*), Travis Bickle (*Taxi Driver*), and every lead character in *Goodfellas* are *not* likeable. You can create an unlikeable character, but if you push away the audience, it needs to be for a reason. Examples of movies with antiheroes include *Mad Max*, *The Crow*, *Dirty Harry*, and *Léon: The Professional*.

Was Robert De Niro's character in *Raging Bull* just misunderstood? Nope, he was a bastard from top to bottom! Fascinating character though, and we can't take our eyes off him. Why? Because movie bad guys get to do everything we don't get to do in our real lives!

You want people to pay $10 to see your movie? Give them memorable characters by showing real people — living and breathing people — that each member of the audience would be willing to pay $10 to see for 90 minutes in the theater. The audience must be willing to take a ride with someone in your movie.

Just how does a writer almost guarantee that the characters he or she creates will pass the "intriguing" test? Even though many of you will be writing about people you already know, it doesn't hurt to understand what constitutes an interesting character. A character can be a good or bad person. Not everyone may like the character, but he or she must be interesting enough to gain the audience's attention and keep them interested.

Let's first talk about two devices that most often work for making your character interesting (but only if these devices are pertinent to your story):

- Characters with disabilities (e.g., *Rain Man*, *The Miracle Worker*, or the devastating *The Elephant Man*).

- Characters in some type of danger or emotional or physical pain (e.g., *127 Hours*, *Cape Fear*, or *Saw*).

For example, if your story opens with a blind person, even without ever hearing the person say a word, the audience will care about him or her immediately. That is not to say that the audience's opinion of the person will not change after they get to know him or her, because it might. That device will only work temporarily. The takeaway from this is that a character with a disability will almost certainly garner sympathy from the reader/audience. This will only work for a short time; eventually, the character has to do more to earn the reader's sympathy. An example here would be Al Pacino's character in *Scent of a Woman* — a great movie where the climax was the famous blind tango scene.

If your story opens with a woman running from a man in a ski mask, even though we may not know anything about her, we are already rooting for her to escape the madman and make it to safety. Though this is a great tactic to instantly get your reader to identify with a character, it will only work for a short time. Eventually, she will escape the madman (if she is the protagonist), and the audience will want to know what else you have to offer in your story. They want to know why they should continue liking and caring about the character.

What you want are characters who are gray — meaning they aren't black and white. Think about real life and how everyone has problems and complications in their lives. Even with comedies, people want the hero to have a little bit of bastard in him; for example, Humphrey Bogart in *Casablanca*. When the movie opens Bogart's character is selfish beyond belief; he is only out for himself and a buck. By the end of the movie, he jeopardizes his own life helping the freedom fighter, Laszlo, get out of town. Even bad guys can have good moments in a movie.

Another example is when Frankenstein admires flowers with a little girl before he accidentally drowns her in the movie *Frankenstein*.

Sometimes having a character want something that we ourselves want (a universal desire) is enough for us to like them as well.

2. Character Identification

You want to create character identification, which is the psychological relationship between the character and the reader/audience. You want the audience to see themselves in the character portrayed on the big screen.

If someone tells you how much a character you created reminded him or her of a brother, or a mother, you have succeeded at creating character identification because the character resonates with the person. He or she can recognize that character as someone he or she has known in his or her own life. The person could even recognize himself or herself in the character. One of the highest compliments any writer can hear is: "Your movie brought back memories of my brother. He died last year." Or, "Your movie meant so much to me. My mother was the same way."

3. Character Biographies

When casting your story, you will compile a list of the prominent characters and the roles they will play. This is called your *master list of characters*. Characters with walk-on roles such as waiters, drivers, doormen, etc., need not be a part of your master list of characters.

Using the case study screenplay as an example (see Appendix), here are the principal characters in *Pictures of Baby Jane Doe*:

- Horace is the lead character. He's in his 20s. He's a person who doesn't hold jobs for long periods of time. What does he want? To help Jane change her life and to help her live to see another day. He also wants to be a writer.

- Jane, the second main character, is a woman in her 20s with a Hollywood smile. She is addicted to drugs and on occasion, works the streets to make money to feed her addiction. What does Jane want? She wants to make her dad, and those around her, happy but struggles because of her own vices.

- Lucinda, a secondary character, is also a drug addict and a close friend of Jane's. What does Lucinda want? She has her own agenda and likes to be a bad influence on those around her. She's trouble.

- Vince (another secondary character) is Jane's father and wants what is best for Jane.

This concludes a minor sketch of the prominent characters and what each hopes to achieve. Knowing these goals beforehand will allow you to move each scene forward in your writing as you push the characters in the direction of their goals. (See Worksheet 3 for a mini character sketch.)

It is a known fact that the more you know about a character, the more interesting the character is to the reader/audience. This proves true in real life as well as in fiction. For that reason, when fleshing out your characters in a more detailed character biography, it is to your advantage to reveal as much about the character as you can. (See Worksheet 4 for a detailed character biography.)

It's the job of the screenwriter to have the characters attempt to accomplish their goals with much resistance. Obviously, if the characters were to accomplish their goals on the first try, there would be no story.

The protagonist of your story is the character whose motivation drives the main story. This is also the character who should be sympathetic and interesting.

A detailed character biography is a great way to get an up-close and personal look at your characters and how they will play an integral part in your story. Although there are numerous ways of going about defining your characters, you may find that creating a simple sketch is all that is necessary to get you started.

Worksheet 3 is a basic sketch. If you really want to know your characters, you may want to delve into the characters' backgrounds. Worksheet 4 is a more detailed character biography. It will help you flesh out the more intimate details of your characters, which in turn will help you get to know them better. If you know your characters well, it will be apparent in your script, and it will give your eventual audience character identification — you want to connect with your audience.

WORKSHEET 3
Mini Character Sketch

Name of character: _____

Age: _____

Who this person is: _____
_____

Physical description: _____
_____

Occupation: _____
_____

Residence: _____
_____

Hobbies: _____
_____

What he or she wants: _____
_____

Greatest strength: _____
_____

Greatest flaw: _____
_____

Why readers like
or dislike this character: _____
_____

There are many character biography templates that you can find online. Each one will be different; for example, at Columbia College students break down characters into three categories of traits: physical, socio-economical, and psychological. Paul Peditto's model (see Worksheet 4) has two categories: exterior and interior. The exterior is the appearance that everyone shows to the world through their jobs, families, hobbies, and educations. The interior view is often contradictory because it's what we *need* and *want*. Oftentimes this contradicts what appears to be what we're about — meaning what *is* and what *appears* to be.

WORKSHEET 4
Detailed Character Biography

Full name: _____

Occupation: _____

Residence: _____

Birth date: _____ Place of birth: _____

Physical Features

Body type: _____ Height: _____

Weight: _____ Measurements: _____

Clothing sizes: _____ Hair color: _____

Hair length: _____ Eye color: _____

Handedness: _____

Most valuable physical asset: _____

Vocal tone: _____

Birthmarks or scars noticeable to the general public (describe where they are located on the character's body): _____

_____

Hidden birthmarks or scars (describe where they are located on the character's body):

_____

If the character's features were destroyed beyond recognition, is there any other way of identifying his or her body? _____

_____

Does the character have any tattoos and/or body piercings (describe where they are located on the character's body)? _____

Does the character wear any identifiable jewelry? _____

Childhood

Describe the area where the character was raised: _____

_____

Describe the type of home life the character had as a child: _____

_____

Childhood friends and enemies: _____

_____

Childhood activities, hobbies, and sports played: _____

_____

Art and/or music training: _____

_____

Family

Father's full name: _____

Mother's full name including maiden name: _____

Brothers' names: _____

Sisters' names: _____

Other relatives: _____

List all current knowledge of family addresses, spouses, children, birth dates, schooling, and any important incidents that only the character and his or her family would remember:

_____

_____

_____

_____

_____

Schooling

Grade school: _____

Junior high school: _____

High school: _____

College: _____

University: _____

Other schooling: _____

Military service: _____

Graduate work: _____

Life Experience

Who are the role models of the character now, and who were they when the character was a child?

_____

_____

Who had, or what event had, the most personal direct influence on the character's life?

_____

_____

What is the character's code of honor? _____

Is there anything the character absolutely will not do? _____

Does the character have any fears or phobias? _____

What are the character's weaknesses? _____

At present, what is the most important thing to the character? _____

To what lengths would the character go to achieve a goal? ___

What was the character's greatest failure? _____

What was the character's greatest triumph? _____

What does the character do best? _____

How does the character relax? _____

What does the character do that he or she would like to improve? _____

_____

Personal

Best friend: _____

Worst enemy: _____

Current girlfriend, boyfriend, or spouse: _____

Is the character's girlfriend, boyfriend, or spouse an occasional date or a steady partner? _____

Is the character's girlfriend, boyfriend, or spouse a lover (i.e., physically intimate)? _____

How does the character's girlfriend, boyfriend, or spouse view him or her? _____

Is the character pure (i.e., virginal)? _____

Does the character consider himself or herself to be attractive?

_____

Describe the character's one great love affair: _____

_____

Give a description of the place the character lives, including a floor plan (if possible):

_____

_____

_____

_____

What is the character's general reaction to an attractive individual who lets him or her know he or she is available? _____

_____

List bad habits: _____

List personal quirks: _____

List vices: _____

List good qualities: _____

List favorite color, food, clothing, weapons, drink, books, and music: _____
_____
_____

What morals does the character have? _____

Describe the character's general personality: _____
_____

Describe any personal tragedy (include the year it happened, the event, and the people involved):
_____
_____

Who is the last person the character would like to see? Why? What would be his or her reaction to seeing that person? _____
_____

Occupation and Skills

What made the character choose his or her present occupation? _____
_____

How do the character's relatives and friends view his or her present occupation?
_____
_____

What did he or she do before his or her current job (list odd or interesting jobs)? How long did the character work at each job? _____
_____

Describe any traumatic experiences in the character's present occupation that have affected him or her deeply in some way: _____
_____

What has the character done that was considered "outstanding" in his or her chosen occupation?
_____

How does the character get along with others in the same occupation? _____
_____

How important is success for the character? _____

What are the character's long-term goals? _____

What is the character willing to do to obtain these goals? _____
_____

Travel

Does the character get seasickness, airsickness, or motion sickness in a vehicle or riding on an animal's back? _____

Does the character like riding animals (e.g., horses, camels)? _____

Any fears about traveling? _____

What steps would the character take to travel overseas? _____
_____

What sort of general equipment would the character take (excluding personal items such as clothing)?
_____
_____

List anything else about the character that you think is important:
_____
_____
_____
_____
_____
_____

Chapter Three

Planning Your Story

An outline is a blueprint for your story, pinpointing what will happen when, where, and why. This blueprint will aid you in structuring your story so that specific events happen at the right time for the most dramatic effect.

Crafting an outline for your screenplay is an excellent way to see your story at a glance before you begin writing. You can flesh out your ideas and choose dramatic events that will eventually work their way into your screenplay.

Some screenwriters will swear by outlines while others just write the story and see where it ends. This is a choice of *process*. It's up to you to decide what process works best for you. If you feel you need to know the story ahead of time, then yes, go ahead and outline it. If you don't want to know every twist and turn of the story, then don't outline it. An apt analogy would be taking a vacation and working out every day's itinerary — some people want order, while others want to be surprised and not know every road they're about to drive down.

The best thing I can say about an outline is that I was once able to write a first draft in less than two weeks working from an outline. The story was plotted from beginning to end, and all that remained was for me to write the individual scenes. In saying that, if this is your first screenplay, it might be a good idea to outline your story completely before you begin writing. Depending on the writer, it could take weeks, even months, just to figure out what happens in advance.

As far as how long it takes to write the script, there is no single answer to that question. Professionals, under the gun, can rewrite an entire script in a week or two. Some take scripts from the idea stage to the final copy in three months. And there are some who have taken three years and are still not happy with it. It depends on the individual.

1. The Three-Act Structure

In outlining a story, many screenwriters work with a three-act structure which could simply be called the beginning or setup (i.e., Act 1), the middle or confrontation (i.e., Act 2), and the ending or resolution (i.e., Act 3).

During the first act, all of the major characters in the story are introduced, setting is established, and the conflict that will move the story is introduced. The Syd Field system calls for *sequences*, similar to chapters in a book. The first ten minutes are the most critical. The reason? The readers won't go past this point if you can't capture their attention and grab them with the writing.

How do you capture the readers' attention? What you want in the first ten pages is to establish the protagonist and key characters, tone, world (i.e., setting), and the beginning of the conflict. For example, think about what gets established in the first ten minutes of *The Godfather*. The setting is the wedding. We meet all the key characters, the tone (i.e., drama), the world (i.e., Mafia in the 1940s), and the beginning of the conflict.

In the second act, your protagonist will face obstacle after obstacle and be forced to rethink his or her original goal and/or grow as a result, if he or she wants to succeed. The first half of the second act is defined by rising action. The midpoint is the break. The back end is the descent into the low point or maximum danger point, where your protagonist faces a huge setback, and it seems as if all hope is lost. This is usually located at the end of Act 2. This is the "do or die" moment, and we find out if your protagonist will accomplish his or her goal or not.

Act 3 is the climax. It traditionally has a resolution (though not always) and is the payoff to everything set up in Act 1.

2. Bullet-Point Scene Descriptions

Your goal when outlining your story using bullet-point scene descriptions is to come up with at least 100 bullet points, theorizing that each bullet will translate into one and a half to two pages of the script. (For an example of a script, see the Appendix as well as the websites Drew's Script-O-Rama and Simply Scripts.)

- Scene 1. Bill kills Bob with a beer bottle.
- Scene 2. The cops show up at the bar to ask questions.
- Scene 3. Bill packs suitcases; gets ready to leave town.

After you gather your bullet-point scene descriptions, you will read them over and begin revising as necessary. Once you are at a place where you really like the way the story plays out, you can then move on to the most exciting part of all: writing the story.

When you are penning your outline, excluding a few rare exceptions, each scene should either reveal character or move the story forward.

3. Using the Index Card Method

The old index card system would have you lay out the cards on a large table, then take hours or even days to move the cards around, take them out, and add to them, to see the entire movie there in front of you. Now this method can be done using computer software; the index card option is included in the *Final Draft* software. You can "card out" on the computer, move scenes around, even delete them just like with paper index cards.

The index card system was established by Syd Field, who is a screenwriting book institution unto himself. For more information about Field, check out his website: www.sydfield.com.

Remember, there is always more than one way to accomplish a goal. If you feel the index card method may work for you, by all means, give that method a try.

4. Flesh out the Story

When a student comes to me with a story idea, we attempt to flesh it out. I do this generally in two ways:

1. **Character biographies:** If the student has an idea about the characters in his or her story, we flesh them out with full page biographies about who they are (see Chapter 2). The student can draw out protagonist, antagonist, and lead secondary characters. Once the person does this, he or she can expand them to include the world (i.e., setting) of the movie. Do we see the lead character at home? What's his or her home life like? How about life at school or at work? How about with his or her spouse or girlfriend or boyfriend? Sketch the character, see the world the movie will be showing, and then work toward writing scenes.

2. **Story development:** Some students don't have characters in mind, but they have a vague idea of the story they want to write. I try to flesh this out with them, writing step outlines, which look like this:

   1. INT. BAR — NIGHT

   Colonel Mustard kills Miss Scarlett with a lead pipe.

   2. EXT. CAR — CONTINUOUS

   Colonel Mustard drives off into the night, leaving mustard stains in his wake.

In other words, we are breaking down the movie scene by scene in a very rough way. You should *not* attempt to tell the whole story in one fell swoop. It takes days, even weeks to get your head around the idea. Take your time, and chip away at the movie. Try to get the first ten pages in your mind in rough scenes. Then the first act, then to the midpoint, and finally to the end.

It's okay if you have only random, out-of-sequence scenes in mind. Write them down. You can work to connect them later. This is how you write the movie. It's like the spine of a human being; you add the connective tissue.

One last note about outlining. The basic building blocks of a movie include (in the following order):

- The *beat*, which is defined as the smallest actable moment.

- The *scene*. There are usually more than 100 scenes in a feature-length movie.

- The *sequence*, which are set pieces encompassing many scenes (e.g., the wedding scene in *The Godfather*, the rescue of Morpheus scene in *The Matrix*).

- The *act*. Three acts is the usual; although some say that's an antiquated measure (note that TV is different).

- The *movie* (made up of your three acts, 100 or more scenes, and many, many beats).

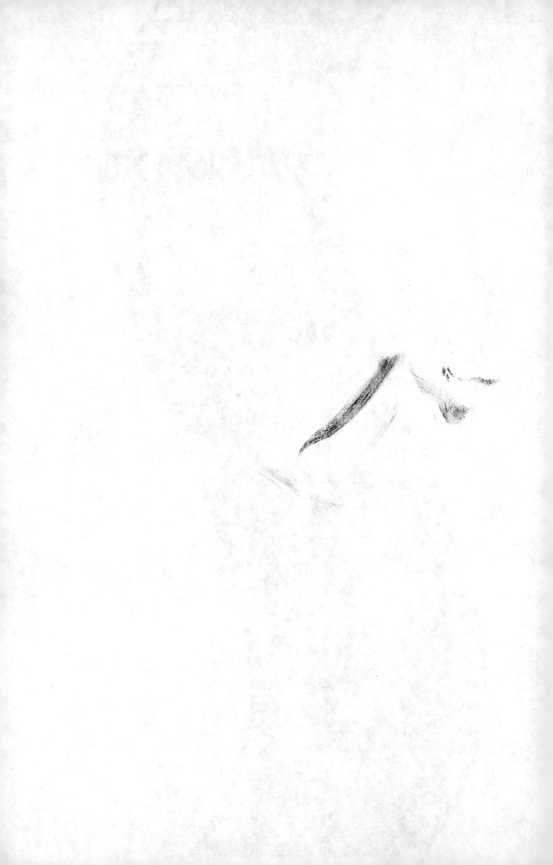

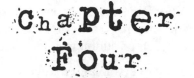

Chapter Four

Writing Your Screenplay

What's the difference between writing a book and writing a screenplay? Books are written to be *read*, and screenplays are written to be *seen*.

Because of strict structural and length requirements, the screenplay version of your life story will cut to the meat of your memoir and highlight what's most important. Movies are juxtaposed *images*; they are about the visual. The screenwriter's job is to join images together to evoke emotion in the audience. In a screenplay, audience members only know what they can see with their eyes or hear spoken from other characters. No background information is given unless it is spoken directly by one of the characters.

Books have dialogue, action, descriptions of emotions and thoughts, and lots of descriptions of people and places. Details of clothes, furniture, weather, hairstyles, body parts, even smells of food and other things are all highlighted in the book medium. It's why so many screen adaptations of books feel leaden and slow.

Another thing that sets these two mediums apart is that screenplays are confined to one page equaling one minute of screen time; therefore, by necessity, a script should be 90 to 120 pages. A novel can be

250 pages or more. A book has no time constraints, so the story can be as long as needed, which means book writers have the luxury of revealing more incidents, characters, subplots, and reflective thoughts.

As different as the book version and the screenplay version may be, the one thing they do have in common is the same underlying story, just presented differently. To reiterate the point about the difference in the amount of description in a book versus a screenplay, Sample 1 shows the difference in writing styles between screenplays and books. Pay close attention to the way the room and people are described in the book versus how they are described in the screenplay version.

1. Establish a Writing Schedule

Dorothy Parker, the American poet and short story writer, said it best: "I hate writing; I love having written." If you are serious about completing your first screenplay, you will want to devise a writing schedule to which you can commit. In designing your schedule, you will need to choose the number of days you will write, the time of day at which you will write, and how many pages you plan to complete each time. Creating a schedule for writing your outline will help you stay focused.

Set a deadline for completing your screenplay. Would you like to have a completed screenplay by your birthday? Christmas? Labor Day? No problem. All you have to do is make a schedule and commit to making it happen.

It's always better to write every day. But what if you can't? Should you *not* write? Of course you should write! The key is *energy*. You have to come at writing with good energy. It doesn't matter if you write in Starbucks every night or on your back porch on Saturdays only, just set a time and be prepared to write.

Your writing schedule may look something like this:

You will write Monday through Friday between the hours of 6:00 p.m. and 8:00 p.m. (if you are an evening writer) with a goal of 4 pages a day. According to this formula, you will have a 100-page screenplay in five weeks, which is no small accomplishment! You may be thinking, "What if I can't come up with that much writing?" Just write something, regardless of how bad it might be. This will keep you in the practice of following your writing schedule. The goal is to get it written; then get it right.

SAMPLE 1
Differences between a Script
and a Book

Book:

In Michelle's living room, daylight seeped through the closed mini blinds and reflected off the shiny floors and polished furniture. Except for the mushroom white director's chair, every piece of furniture was a lustrous black.

Michelle stood at the front door and waited for Sarah Jane to tower down the hall.

"Have you ever been so angry with someone that you plotted their murder?" Sarah Jane asked as she moseyed through the front door and removed her coat.

"Not lately."

Screenplay:

```
INT. MICHELLE'S APARTMENT - DAY

Glitzy pad, every piece of furniture shines a lustrous black.
Michelle and Sarah Jane chat in the spacious living room.

                    SARAH JANE
          Ever think about killing someone?

                    MICHELLE
          Not lately.
```

Book:

Sarah Jane was a legal secretary, almost six feet tall, thirty-five, and the slimmest of the slim. With purple being her color of choice, it was more of an obsession. It was her boyfriend's favorite color and she relished wearing it, even basked in it.

Sarah Jane peeled off her boots, folded her arms, and cuddled her forearms. "It's cold in here."

Screenplay:

```
Peeling off her purple boots...

                    SARAH JANE
          It's cold in here.
```

Book:

Michelle closed the window then headed toward the kitchen. Sarah Jane made a beeline right behind her and slumped down into the kitchen chair, sitting on one folded leg.

"I was *so* mad at him, Michelle."

"But you are always angry with him."

Screenplay:

Michelle moves into the

KITCHEN

Sarah joins her.

> SARAH JANE
> I'm mad at him.

> MICHELLE
> You're always mad at him.

> SARAH JANE
> It's different this time.

> MICHELLE
> How?

> SARAH JANE
> I'm thinking, kill him, burn his building
> down.

Book:

"Trust me. This time was different. I could not reach him for two days. It was like he disappeared from the face of the earth, and I was fuming. I was so mad, I had smoke coming from my nose and ears. I'm serious Michelle, I was really going to kill him."

Michelle laughed, because she knew Sarah Jane was just venting. "How? How were you going to do it?"

"I don't know how, but I was going to kill him and then burn his building down."

Michelle brewed a fresh pot of french vanilla coffee and sat down in the chair across from Sarah Jane.

"Well, I'm so glad you didn't, because I would have missed you when they locked you up."

"At least I wouldn't have to stress out about him anymore."

SAMPLE 1 — Continued

Screenplay:

Laughing, sipping her french vanilla coffee...

                    MICHELLE
        Good idea. No more stress that way.

                  SARAH JANE
        You think I'm kidding.

                    MICHELLE
        Of course you're ...

Michelle looks to Sarah Jane, who doesn't laugh back. The smile vanishes from Michelle's face.

Never revise while you are writing your first draft. In other words, don't keep rewriting the first 30 pages. Your goal is to get the words on the pages and then revise the story to perfection. Some people who stop and revise end up with five perfectly written pages and nothing else. They spend so much time revising the first five pages that they fail to move forward and write a complete story. You should get through the first draft in rough fashion. Push forward even if it means writing "insert funny joke here" and then coming back to it later in the revision process. If you get stuck, just keep moving. Remember, write first and revise second. (See Chapter 5 for more information about revising your story.)

In the first draft you want to say everything that comes to mind. Write it out in full. If it turns out to be 150 pages, you can always reduce the page count later. Say everything you want to say in the first pass-through; there'll be plenty of time for editing later.

2. Tips for Writing Scenes

Writing individual scenes is the meat of what screenwriting is all about and what many people find to be the most fun part of the project.

If you have completed your outline, you should know the plot of your entire story. However, if you have chosen not to work with an outline, you can still begin writing your story scene by scene if you know who and what your story is about.

2.1 Story setup

The first ten pages are about the story setup. They include key characters, tone, setting, and conflict. Your story will begin with a question. Your job as a screenwriter is to write scene after scene until the question of what the story is about is answered.

Where you begin your story sets the tone for the entire script. If your story is about romance, the first scene should hint at that. Scenes exist to advance character or plot.

How do you decide where the story should begin? Your story will begin with a scene that illustrates who the character is and what the story is about. For example, if your chosen story is about what happened to you during your first year at college, a great opening scene might be you saying goodbye to your parents at the airport. Or, you could describe a scene with you arriving at your dorm room and meeting your eccentric new roommate. Right away the audience will know who and what the story is about. This is called the *point of entry*. You pick up a movie at the absolute last moment possible. Get in late, get out early (see section **2.2** for more on this).

Once you have set up your story, your job is to continue writing scene after scene until you reach a logical ending. The journey or the plot of your screenplay is everything that happens along the way or everything that happens while the characters are attempting to accomplish their goals. When nothing happens in the first ten pages of your story and/or when your main character is not identified from the start, your screenplay is dead on arrival.

2.2 Get in late, get out early

The "get in late, get out early" technique is important to novelists and to screenwriters, but especially so for screenwriters. What this simply means is that you begin the scene in the middle of the conversation where the drama is, and end the scene before it turns boring.

You want to cut out getting in and out of cars, knocking on doors, introductions, and small talk that adds up to nothing. You want to get into the scene as late as possible to keep the movie moving. If a wife is looking for her cheating husband, you could show her furious, driving in the car, then cut to her inside the bar looking for him. You don't have to show her parking the car, walking to the front door, opening up the door, and walking inside.

For example, if a character is about to ask his boss for a raise, you could begin the scene at the exact moment when he asks for the raise. Or, you could have him sit down before his boss, and without a word, cut to him coming out of the office, crushed. We can *see* on his face that he didn't get the raise. Most scenes are written like this, but not all.

2.3 Scene setup and payoff

A scene setup is basically background information for a scene that will happen later, making the future scene believable. For example, in *Thelma & Louise*, when Thelma is packing for her road trip, we see her pack her husband's gun, and then give it to her friend, Louise, to keep for her. Later, when Louise uses it to shoot a would-be rapist, we understand where the gun came from, making the scene effective and believable, which gives the audience the payoff. If we had not seen the gun beforehand, we would have had a hard time believing that Louise would carry a gun.

If your scene calls for a character to defend herself against a would-be mugger, we need to know beforehand that she is skilled at self-defense. That information can be conveyed either visually, where we see her learning self-defense, or it could be conveyed verbally when someone asks her about her self-defense training.

2.4 Use present tense action verbs

Screenplays are written in present tense, unlike what you might see in a novel. In a screenplay, you would write, "she opens the drawer and unwraps the gun," not "she opened the drawer and unwrapped the gun." Note that past tense is not used in a screenplay.

Action verbs capture the imagination and give the feeling of immediacy. Use colorful verbs often. For example:

- Don't do: Jimmy is walking slowly down the street
- Do: Jimmy prances down the street.

To clarify, don't use he *is* running, she *is* playing, or they *are* jumping. Instead say, he runs, she plays, or they jump.

2.5 Creative descriptions

Original and colorful descriptions of people and places make for an enjoyable reading experience. A few words which paint an engaging image of a character or place will work better than long-winded prose. For example, a shiny Mercedes is much more effective and specific than a black car. If you were to describe a sexy woman, you might say "a sexy Barbie doll" or "a sex kitten." If you wanted to describe a fancy restaurant, you might say "water costs $10 a bottle here." Though only a few words, such descriptions are effective in crystallizing an accurate image.

When describing characters in your screenplay, don't limit yourself to just their physical attributes. Mention such things as hair length or style, designer clothing, and distinctive personality traits. You want to shoot for the visible essence of the character. To write that the character is 35 years old and wearing jeans tells the reader nothing. Anyone could do that. The following is a good example of a character description from *Bad Santa*, describing the Billy Bob Thornton character:

A wiry, hard-bitten, sunbaked saddlebag of a man, Gin Slagel sits behind his cluttered desk sucking on a filterless Pall Mall. We can hear his intake of breath rattling over and around the phlegm, growths, and polyps that line his embattled trachea. His words come out on an exhaled cloud chamber's worth of smoke …

3. Elements Necessary for Constructing a Scene

The elements that are necessary for constructing a scene include the slugline (scene heading), action, character, dialogue, parenthetical, and transition, which are described in the next few sections.

3.1 Slugline (scene heading)

A slugline (i.e., scene heading) is how you start every scene. It has three parts:

- INT. or EXT. (i.e., interior or exterior)
- Location
- Time of day (night, day, later same day, continuous, etc.)

For example, it would look like this:

INT.   BAR — NIGHT

EXT.   STREET — DAY

Every change in location denotes a new slugline with a change in time or location. If the camera doesn't cut away, characters could walk to the living room and it wouldn't be a new scene at all. If they're in the kitchen and the camera cuts to the living room five minutes later, it's a new slugline.

3.2 Action

Action is the business of what is happening in the scene. This is where you describe exactly what the characters are doing. Are they walking, talking, eating, or making love? For example:

INT.   BAR — NIGHT

A COUPLE drink wine by candlelight.

You want to keep action areas to "what the camera is seeing now"; who is in the shot and what is happening. Keep your descriptions simple, with no more than four or five lines per paragraph.

3.3 Character description

When key characters are introduced for the first time, their first and last names are typed in all capital letters. Key characters get a brief description such as their age or approximate age. A good description of a person can be as simple as "sexy blond" or something along the lines of "she could be a model." When the movie is produced, the viewers will never read the words "sexy blond" or "she could be a model"; instead, they will actually see the sexy blond in full form. The character is only described the first time he or she appears in the story. After that, the character is referred to simply by his or her name. For example:

INT.   BAR — NIGHT

A COUPLE drink wine by candlelight. They are MICKEY MORGAN (35) pretty brunette and JAY MALONE (37) with movie-star looks.

You don't describe unimportant characters. Characters with no dialogue are not named unless they somehow impact plot. Unimportant characters should be given descriptive non-names such as HUNKY BARISTA or POTENTIAL SKANK.

3.4 Dialogue

By definition, the only time you have dialogue in a screenplay is when the image is not enough. Dialogue fills in the gaps of the audience's knowledge, but it's not a substitute for the visual solution. Always look for the visual solution.

In screenplays, because of time constraints, most dialogue is reduced to the best part of the conversation. The "hello" and "how are you" are deleted so that the only dialogue remaining is the heat of the conversation and nothing else.

Writing dialogue is something often debated in terms of whether it can be taught or not. Can I really teach you to be funny? Doubtful. One thing you can do is listen. Use your ears. Hear conversations around you. Hear language.

Understand that good dialogue isn't writing perfect sentences. It's actually non-perfection. Good dialogue is made up of stops and starts, interruptions, half-thoughts, pauses, accents, educational backgrounds, obscenities, and intellect (or lack of it).

The writer should work out dialogue by reading it out loud. It's not going to be perfect the first time. A classic scene in *Mozart* is when Salieri gets his hands on Mozart's original writing and there are *no* corrections on it! The very hand of God had touched Mozart. One thing I can assure you is that you are not Mozart. Dialogue will take several passes to get it right, so don't be afraid to write, and rewrite.

You write dialogue by writing dialogue, which means writing a lot. Some say a writer has to write a million words to write his or her first real word. I say writing good dialogue is a lifelong pursuit, and it will take time. Be patient.

Comedies, in general, are faster with the interchanges and the timing, but quick-moving movies aren't limited to comedies. Look at the Academy Award-winning drama *The Social Network*. It was a 162-page script! That means it should have taken two and a half hours on the screen. It took only two hours because of the incredible speed of the dialogue.

In a screenplay, characters are either saying something or doing something. They talk *or* they move or they talk *and* move. In the book medium, the writer has the luxury of telling the reader what the character is thinking. In screenwriting, everything that needs to be disclosed to the audience is either spoken or it is displayed on the screen. For example, if you wrote a story about a female school-teacher, the way in which you would reveal that information to the audience would be to actually see the character standing in a class-room teaching or grading papers, or for the character herself or some other character in the story to make reference to the fact that she is a teacher. For instance, the character might say to her friend, "I'll scream if I have to grade one more paper."

A great way to write effective dialogue is to have your characters say things that are unexpected. For example, if I were to ask you, "How are you?" Your standard response might be, "Fine." In screenwriting, an exchange like that would be the kiss of death. If your character asks, "How are you?" a more creative response might be "How do I look?" Even better would be showing the character cutting an onion as though she wants to hurt someone, as she says nothing (using the visual solution). Of course, the dialogue needs to fit the character. Ask yourself, what would be the typical response — and then do something totally different.

Keep dialogue to a minimum. Only use what is necessary to advance character or plot. Don't spell out everything in dialogue. Remember that the actors are filling in emotional gaps with body language. Write dialogue with an eye toward subtext. Say it *without* saying it.

Subtext is the key to writing good dialogue. Subtext is the meaning behind the words. The actions of the character and the emotions portrayed in the dialogue create the subtext. Subtext is one of the great things about writing screenplays. You get to be creative in your strategy for revealing information.

Study the works of the best scriptwriters. Read how the greats, such as Quentin Tarantino, Woody Allen, William Goldman, and Paul Schrader write dialogue. Go to the websites Drew's Script-O-Rama or SimplyScripts. Find online sources where you can read TV scripts for series such as *The Wire* or *The Sopranos*.

3.5 Parenthetical

Occasionally, you'll need a parenthetical. This is when you want to describe *how* an actor delivers a line. Any kind of parenthetical de-scription such as laughing, smiling, or coughing should be placed in parentheses and centered directly below the character name. For example, (sarcastically) or (laughing). You will want to limit the amount of direction included in your screenplay; I urge you to use these sparingly. No actor likes to be told how to deliver a line.

MICKEY

(smiling) (pulls out a gun)

Gimme your dough, see!

3.6 Transition

On occasion, you'll need a transition, which indicates a change from one setting to another setting. A transition can also indicate the story is moving to a new time frame.

To show a transition for an abrupt change you will use CUT TO, in capital letters and followed by a colon.

The first words on the page that come after the title page are FADE IN. This is in capital letters and followed by a colon. Fade in is only used once at the beginning of the screenplay.

FADE OUT, with a period after it, is written at the end of the screenplay just before you write THE END.

4. Title of Your Screenplay

The creation of the perfect title may come to you after you have finished writing your screenplay. If you have not yet decided on a title for your screenplay, by the time you finish writing your first draft, you may know what to title your masterpiece so don't fret. The title summarizes your story, so creating it at the end of writing will give it the right name.

Note that your screenplay title may be changed. If you sell your movie, you give up all rights. The studio owns it and can do as they please with it.

5. Title Page

Your screenplay begins with a title page. The text on the title page is centered. It begins with the title of the screenplay followed by the name of the writer. A few inches below that is the mailing address of the writer or the agent. However, if you are using screenwriting software, the placement of text on the title page is done for you.

This Time Will Be Different

Jessie Jamie Coleman

jessiecoleman@someplaceforemail.com
555-555-5555

If you have an agent, his or her contact information would go on the cover. Otherwise, it's just name and contact information of the writer. See Sample 2.

Never include the copyright information because it's assumed you wrote it.

6. Type of Scripts

Before a screenplay becomes a movie, it is considered a *speculation script* or *spec*. It will be read by many people many times over before it ever makes it to the big screen, which is why it is so important that it be easy to read and properly formatted. In addition, because it is a *reader's script*, there are no camera angles, no scene numbers, and very little, if any, direction. In a spec script, you never write in direct camera angles. That is the director's domain.

The second type of script is called a *shooting script*. It has scene numbers and sometimes camera angles.

7. The Importance of the Screenplay Format

The screenplay format may seem strange to the novice screenwriter, but as with any profession, it is something that must be learned as part of the trade. After some practice, the screenwriting format will become second nature to you.

When writing a feature-length screenplay, it is important that you format it correctly if you hope to be taken seriously in this business. The industry is very adamant about this, and how well your script is formatted is used as a gauge for your professionalism as a screenwriter.

Script readers for production companies and screenwriting contests are looking for a reason to *not* read your script, and formatting is one of the first things readers examine. If you can't get the format right, the thinking goes, "how can you tell me a story of value?" They might never read your magnum opus if the formatting is incorrect, so yes, it's important.

There are a few books that contain comprehensive information about formatting. *The Screenwriter's Bible*, by David Trottier, devotes 100 or more pages to the formatting topic. I also strongly suggest using screenwriting software such as *Final Draft*. If you can't afford that, use the free software, *Celtx*, which mimics the industry standard of *Final Draft*.

I cannot stress enough just how important it is to read screenplays if you are serious about writing them professionally. Not only will you learn all the ins and outs of screenplay format, but you will have a lot of fun doing so as you get immersed in the different stories. (See section **8.2** for places to find published screenplays to read.)

The following list includes formatting issues you will need to understand (see the Appendix for an example of a script):

- **Length:** One page of script is equal to one page of screen time. This means that a 120-page screenplay would translate into a 120 minute movie. Screenplays range between 90 to 120 pages. It used to be that the target length for most features was 120 pages. However, over the years, that number has changed and the new target length is between 100 to 110 pages for a drama. Comedies are even shorter with a target length of 90 to 100 pages.

- **Margins:** The margins of a screenplay should be one inch all the way around, except for the left margin. The left margin should be 1.5 inches, which is automatically formatted for you in screenwriting software.

- **Font:** The font should be Courier and set at 12 points.

- **Header:** The header generally includes only the page number followed by a period and begins on page two of the script.

8. Resources for Screenwriting Programs and Published Screenplays

You can find many screenwriting programs that will help you format your script, but it is also important to read published scripts to get a feel for what others have done.

Check out screenwriting blogs such as coauthor Paul Peditto's scriptgodsmustdie.com. Other blogs you should read include:

- Done Deal Professional (donedealpro.com): a compendium of deals currently being made on new scripts.

- John August (johnaugust.com)

- Wordplay (wordplayer.com)

- Scriptshadow (scriptshadow.blogspot.com)

- Trigger Street Labs (labs.triggerstreet.com): an incredible network for new writers.

8.1 Screenwriting software

It bears mentioning that just because you may have the screenwriting software *Final Draft*, *MovieMagic*, or *Celtx*, it does *not* mean you will automatically know how to format. There are rules that go along with the software that the new writer must master. Practice with the software. Read a professional script from SimplyScripts.com and practice typing it into your software so you get a sense of where each element goes. Here is a list of some well-known screenwriting software:

- *Final Draft*

- *Movie Magic Screenwriter*

- *Celtx*

- *MasterWriter*

- *Script It!*

- *Storybase*

8.2 Published screenplays

Research is important in this industry, so make sure you do it! The following is a list of places where you can find published screenplays:

- SimplyScripts (www.simplyscripts.com)

- Drew's Script-O-Rama (www.script-o-rama.com)

- Bookcity Script Shop (www.hollywoodbookcity.com)

- Script City (www.scriptcity.com)

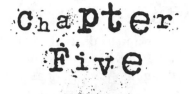

Chapter Five

Revising Your Screenplay

Once you've completed the first draft of your story, it's time to pat yourself on the back. Why not? You deserve it. You began with a blank page and ended with a feature-length screenplay. To go from an idea to a finished screenplay is indeed a victory. After you're done admiring your accomplishment, it's time to begin the second phase of the process: revision.

The revision phase is a great time to give more attention and detail to your description of people and places. Actually, it is a great time to revise everything if needed. Good stories are not written, they are rewritten.

How do you go about revising your story? Some people say you should let your script sit for a week or so before tackling the revisions, which is excellent advice, if you have the patience. Waiting will help you come back to it with fresh ideas and you may see things you missed while writing your script.

1. The Revision Process

The first thing you will want to do is to read through your script from beginning to end; read it out loud, if you can. Make notes along the way of anything that jumps out at you or that you believe needs to be changed.

During the revision process, you may realize that the dialogue you wrote is not as outstanding as you originally thought it was! You may have written your story during an eight-week period, and you may now be reading it in one sitting and seeing inconsistencies.

After the initial read, you will likely see many things you want to change, add, or remove. This is the time when you might decide to change character names, locations, etc. Here is a list of things to look for:

- Read the dialogue from beginning to end and tweak it for cleverness, originality, and unpredictability.

- Is the main character identified in the first five pages?

- Will a reader know what your story is about in the first ten pages?

- Look at your descriptions of people and places. Can they be tweaked for originality and color?

- Are the subplots interesting, and do they tie in with the main story?

- Are all of your scenes needed? Remember that each scene should move the story forward, reveal information, or reveal character.

- Did you get in late, and get out early? There is a purpose for every scene. Do what you have to in the scene then get out.

- Are many of your scenes static, meaning are people sitting and talking instead of doing something (action) and talking?

- Do many of your scenes take place in the same location? Try varying the location. Note that the entire movie *Clerks* was set in two locations: a convenience store and a video store.

- Are the central questions of the story answered at the end?

- Does the title accurately summarize the story?

Another question to ask is: Are your secondary characters pertinent to the story? The rule of thumb is, if a secondary character can be removed from the story without the story being affected, then that character is not necessary to the story. For example, if your story is about a woman who shoots her husband while a nosy neighbor witnesses it and reports it to the police, you cannot remove the nosy neighbor, or you will change the entire dynamic of the story.

You have to do everything possible to make it a commercial property that a producer would be interested in creating. That means not just rewriting it, but getting it proofread, and getting it reviewed by your trusted "inner circle" of readers. This could either consist of friends or a professional script consultant (see Chapter 6). Get feedback then proceed with the rewrite. You may have to repeat this process several times before your script is ready to be sent to industry professionals.

There will never be just one way to revise a story. What matters most is that in the end you craft and complete a well-written and marketable story that readers will love to read and filmmakers will want to produce.

Chapter Six

Script Draft Review and Feedback

You've just finished the first draft of your script. Before you start to rewrite, you need to let it rest for a few days to get some perspective. You also need to seek out a trusted inner circle to read it and give you some feedback for the rewrite — and no, your mother probably doesn't count as inner circle material!

There are online resources and message boards where you can connect with other writers such as the terrific resource Trigger Street Labs (http://labs.triggerstreet.com). There are also mega-services such as ScriptShark that are certainly well-established, but the drawback is that your reader will be completely anonymous. You'll never know him or her, and you'll never know if the reader is truly qualified to give opinions on your script.

Before launching your screenplay into the marketplace, it's important that it is as good as it can be. Unfortunately, because you are the writer, it's difficult for you to judge it objectively. Script consultants can provide a valuable service to the newbie screenwriter. A good analyst can point out your strengths and weaknesses, enabling you to create a marketable product. However, locating legitimate, helpful, and reasonably priced analysis is where the challenge lies. Do your research before picking a script consultant. Seek out the opinions of others about who they use as trusted professional script consultants.

Before shelling out your hard-earned cash, I suggest you begin by asking people within your circle of friends, family, and associates. Granted, unless they are in the industry, they will not be able to critique your script from a professional screenwriting perspective, but they can tell you if they like your characters, if they find the story interesting, and if the dialogue sounds realistic and intriguing. Their feedback may prove extremely helpful.

Some people will say that your friends, family members, and associates are not qualified to offer feedback on your story. They *are* qualified in that they can tell you what they like and don't like. These same people critique movies all the time. However, be sure they're being honest and telling you the truth, not just saying they like everything you did!

After giving your script to your circle of readers, ask them what they thought of it. Be a good listener and take notes about what they tell you. Don't interrupt and try to explain things the readers don't understand. If the readers don't understand, realize that there is a flaw in the story and that you need to rewrite the problem area. Don't take criticism personally. It's about making your story better, so listen!

Even after having your circle of readers review it for you, you still might want to have a professional look at it for you. My advice is to see if you can have someone you know recommend a consultant.

If you are interested in other analysts, screenwriting magazines often have lists of experts eager and ready to serve you. Screenwriting magazines are inundated with script consultants advertising their services. Some are okay and others are better. If you use any of the analysts from magazines, I suggest you research them thoroughly. Note that you don't get to ask the script consultant anything, unless it's a small operation in which the person reading your script will respond to your emails.

You can research consultants by doing a Google search, looking at their websites, comparing prices, reading testimonials, and going to screenwriting message boards for reviews of consultants. *Creative Screenwriting Magazine* also has a special consultant's edition that is very comprehensive.

On average, a script consult (basic service) will cost $100 to $150. A detailed critique with lined notes will cost $250 and up. Hiring a highly respected script consultant, such as Linda Seger, can cost you $1,200 or more depending on the level of review you want for your script.

Chapter Seven

Selling Your Story

You've finished writing your life story into a screenplay. You've had it critiqued and you have revised it numerous times. It is as good as it's going to get, so now what? The next step is to protect your work by copyrighting and/or registering it; then you need to get your script into the right person's hands so the world can eventually see your movie!

1. Copyright

It is of the utmost importance to copyright your story in the US with the Copyright Office and/or to register your screenplay with the Writers Guild of America (WGA) or Canada (WGC).

How long does a copyright last in the US? The term of copyright for a particular work depends on several factors, including whether it has been published, and, if so, the date of first publication. As a general rule, for works created after January 1, 1978, copyright protection lasts for the life of the author plus an additional 70 years. For an anonymous work, a pseudonymous work, or a work made for hire, the copyright endures for a term of 95 years from the year of its first publication or a term of 120 years from the year of its creation, whichever expires first. For works first published prior to 1978, the term will vary depending on several factors. To determine the length of copyright protection for a particular work, consult Chapter 3 of the Copyright Act (title 17 of the *United States Code*). More information on the term of copyright can be found in Circular 15a, *Duration of Copyright*, and Circular 1, *Copyright Basics*.

There is one drawback to having your screenplay copyrighted by snail mail; sometimes, it can take several months before you receive your registration number from the Copyright Office. However, you can copyright automatically with the Library of Congress at www.copyright.gov. Registration is instant.

In Canada, copyright exists automatically when you create an original piece of work and it exists for the creator's lifetime plus 50 years. However, getting a certificate of registration from the Canadian Intellectual Property Office will provide you with evidence that your writing is protected by copyright, and you can prove in a court of law that you have ownership of the work.

At the time of this book's printing, the price for copyrighting in the US (www.copyright.gov) is $35.00 USD (online submission) or $65.00 USD (hard copy submission). In Canada, at the Canadian Intellectual Property Office, (www.cipo.ic.gc.ca), the cost ranges from $50.00 to $65.00 CAD for the certificate of registration (remember, copyright is automatic and therefore free). The price for registering your screenplay with the WGA West (www.wgawregistry.org) is $20.00 USD ($10.00 USD for members). The price for registering your screenplay with the WGA East (www.wgaeast.org/script_registration) is $10.00 USD for members and $25.00 USD for non-members. At the WGC, (www.wgc.ca), registration costs $22.60 online or $25.00 CAD by mail for members; $39.55 CAD online and $40.00 by mail for non-members.

2. The Difference between Optioning and Selling Your Script

When you option a script, you're agreeing to give it to a producer to pitch, sell, and shop for an agreed-upon period of time and for an agreed-upon amount of money. The producer is leasing the script, not buying it. You get the script and all the rights back when the option agreement expires. In this way, you could make money on a script and never have it see the light of a movie screen.

When you sell a screenplay, you are selling *all* rights to your screenplay. If you stay with the project and do a second draft and/or a revision, you are considered to have work-for-hire status; you are a mercenary on your own movie. Producers can fire you should they choose, and they can bring on other writers because the property (i.e., script) belongs to them.

New writers should check the Writers Guild of America website (www.wga.org) or the Writers Guild of Canada (www.wgc.ca) to research writer protections, pay scales, and more. It is recommended that you register your script at the WGA, WGC, or copyright it through the Library of Congress or the Canadian Intellectual Property Office *before* you send out your script.

3. How to Sell Your Story

First thing to ask when selling a script is: Who is my target market? To whom should I sell this work?

Keep in mind that you are not on the lookout for several agents, managers, or producers to like your work, although it would be nice. You only need one person to help you get your foot in the door of the movie industry. The key is to find the right person at the right time.

When screenwriter Antwone Fisher met with movie producer Todd Black about producing his autobiographical screenplay, Black told him, "I'm going to help you get your story made." Black went on to say, "It will not be easy, but I will do what I can." Black was the catalyst for bringing *Antwone Fisher* to the big screen.

Before embarking on any of the following strategies for marketing your screenplay, don't be afraid to study the marketplace and find out who's buying what. Read the trades such as *Variety* and *The Hollywood Reporter* and visit Done Deal Professional (www.donedealpro.com) for the latest spec script sales. Be a student of how people get their movies made. Study. Learn. Be patient. Be proactive. Never take no for an answer.

3.1 Strategy 1: Connect with the people you know in the industry

Make a list of people you know in the business. Make a list of people you know who know people. Relationships are what Hollywood is all about. Think "six degrees of separation." Brainstorm. Be energetic in pursuit of anyone who can help put your script into the right hands.

Cold calling is never as effective as inside sales so ask yourself: Who do I know? Give them the script first. You only get one shot with professionals, so make sure the script is ready to go out before you call in favors.

3.2 Strategy 2: Write a query letter

You have probably heard and read about the query letter quite a few times, and although many people will tell you it is a waste of time, for some, it continues to work and will continue to work.

Without a referral or a connection to someone in the industry, a query letter could be your entryway into the screenwriting industry. A query letter says: I'm a screenwriter who has written a story which may be of interest to you.

Are the odds great for you succeeding with a query letter? Nope. But it's a strategy, one of many that you as an unknown screenwriter can use. Control what you can control.

Avoid negativity and uncertainty in your query letter. Be positive and confident, and do not add words such as "hopefully" or "maybe." Your query letter should contain a concise first paragraph that describes the movie. If you have a killer premise, it will interest the reader. So will a killer hook. If your movie is a comedy, write a funny query letter.

The second paragraph should describe why you are the one to write this movie. Present your professional writing credits and mention if you have placed in a screenwriting competition, or optioned a script. In addition, if you previously met the person you're querying at a seminar or other event, feel free to mention that in your query letter.

Some people will say that effective query letters will capture the attention of an industry professional, which is true, if your story happens to be what he or she is interested in; otherwise, it's a crap shoot. Not everyone likes the same stories. Make sure you target an agent who actually makes sales in the genre under which your story would be classified. To find the right people to send your query letter to, pick up a copy of the *Hollywood Creative Directory*, which has a list of every production company and agent in the business.

Note that the query letter isn't about you; it's about selling your story to an agent. What's in it for the agent? Why should he or she be interested? The agent doesn't know you, so boil down your idea to its most commercial and exciting elements. Write the concept, and write the hook. Tell the plot in broad, bold detail. Tighten it. Read the summary paragraph as a pitch, out loud, and to everyone you know. What excites people about your story? What bores people? Start again. Tighten it up. Agents believe that if you can't write the hell out of a one-page query letter, you probably can't write a screenplay. Put yourself in the shoes of the agent. Imagine the stack of queries he or she must go through each week.

Sample 3 is a query letter that was used to garner reading requests from several literary agents.

Do not mass mail your query letter. Make sure each query letter you send identifies each agent, by addressing them by their proper name and title. Remember to include a self-addressed stamped envelope or postcard so you get a reply.

Send out letters in groups of 20 and make a list of Group A, Group B, and so forth. Mail to Group A first and as the rejections come in check them off the list. Stay updated. Don't give it more than four to six weeks before you send your second wave (i.e., Group B).

If you've written a good query letter, ideally 5 or so agents out of 100 will ask to see your script. If, after the first couple of groups, no one asks to see the script, you need to rework your query letter.

Interested agencies will ask you to sign a *release form*, which allows them to read your script. This is standard practice. Send back the release with the script, and wait for the agent's response.

3.2a Research the market

After you have written your perfect query letter, it's time to find agents and producers who may be interested in your story. (In section **3.2b**, you will find a list of agents and producers; this information may change at any time.)

To increase your chances of locating a producer interested in your story, research will be necessary. You should first begin by creating a list of movies that are somewhat similar in story or in genre to the story you have created. From there, you want to find the names of

SAMPLE 3
Query Letter

Date

Your name
Your address

Dear Ms. Agent:

I have recently completed a feature-length screenplay which may be of interest to you. The title is *The Ghost of Charlie Weiss*, and it could be categorized as romantic suspense.

I have written several spec scripts, mostly in the genre of romantic suspense, and several have advanced in screenplay competitions.

The Ghost of Charlie Weiss
Three Beautiful Redheads — Three Motives — One Murder

Tapping into the common desire to be someone else, if only for a short time, *The Ghost of Charlie Weiss* explores what happens when a woman, bored with her humdrum existence, dyes her hair red, takes on the persona of her late sister, and ends up becoming one of three red-haired suspects to a murder.

After the murder of her beloved sister and parents, a quiet and warm-hearted office worker, Jessica Weiss is in search of an escape. A few sessions with her psychologist propel her to the realization that the excitement she seeks is a new life, the life of her late sister. With a daring wish to continue the wild life of her late sister, she colors her hair red and dares to reinvent herself. With this new persona comes a different type of experience, including becoming one of three suspects to a murder.

If this screenplay interests you, I would be happy to send you a copy.

Very truly yours,

(Insert your signature)
(Print your name below the signature so it is legible.)

the producers who worked on each movie. You can do this by visiting the Internet Movie Database (www.imdb.com) and typing in the name of the movie. A list of credits will usually follow, including the names of all of the producers who worked on the film.

For example, let's say you wrote a horror movie and you have decided to go the query letter route. Try to target agents who might respond to the horror genre. Find out which agents have sold horror movie scripts. Get their names and agency information. Target production companies too. Go to www.donedealpro.com and subscribe. Pick up a copy of *Hollywood Creative Directory*. It can't be stressed enough how important it is to target companies that are selling your genre.

3.2b List of agents, managers, and production companies

The following list contains script agents, managers, and production companies interested in getting pitches via email or regular mail from unknown or new screenwriters. I have only listed the company names and their websites. Please visit each website for detailed submission instructions.

- AEI Productions (www.aeionline.com)
- Affinity Artists Agency (www.affinityartists.com)
- The Alpern Group (www.alperngroup.com)
- Burton & Robinson Talent Agency (www.burtonrobinsonagency.com)
- Camelot Entertainment (www.camelotent.com)
- Cary Kozlov Literary Representation (www.ckliterary.webs.com)
- The Charlotte Gusay Literary Agency (www.gusay.com)
- Circle of Confusion (www.circleofconfusion.com)
- Concept Entertainment (www.conceptentertainment.biz)
- Craig Anderson Productions (CAP) (www.cappix.com)
- Destiny Pictures (www.destinypictures.biz)
- Epic Level Entertainment (www.epiclevel.com)
- Epiphany Pictures (www.epiphanypictures.com)

- Evatopia (www.evatopia.com)

- Fierce Entertainment (www.fierceentertainment.com)

- The Filmtrix Agency (www.filmtrix.com)

- Gallagher Literary (www.gallagherliterary.com)

- The Gary-Paul Agency (www.thegarypaulagency.com)

- Hays Media LLC (www.haysmedia.net)

- Josselyne Herman & Associates (JHA) (www.jhamanagement.com)

- Madhouse Entertainment (www.madhouseent.net)

- Neo Art & Logic (www.neoartandlogic.com)

- New School Media (www.newschoolmedia.net)

- Objective Entertainment (www.objectiveent.com)

- PMA Literary & Film Management, Inc. (www.pmalitfilm.com)

- Red Hen Productions (www.redhenprods.com)

- Taylor Lane Productions (www.taylorlaneproductions.com)

- Topp Drawer Talent (www.toppdrawer.com)

3.3 Strategy 3: Enter screenplay competitions

Any industry professional or writer will tell you that placing in a prestigious screenwriting competition can launch a writing career. Screenwriting contests are a popular option to get a little attention that can be done inexpensively without the need of industry help.

Screenplay competitions are wonderful exposure because many times simply placing in one of these competitions can capture the attention of agents, managers, and producers, which is exactly what you want.

Your challenge as a writer is to place in or win these competitions. If you decide to enter your screenplay in any of the following competitions, visit their websites and follow the entry instructions to the letter:

- Nicholl Fellowships in Screenwriting (www.oscars.org/awards/nicholl)

- Sundance Screenwriters Lab
  (www.sundance.org/programs/screenwriters-lab)

- The Austin Screenplay Competition
  (www.austinfilmfestival.com/new/screenplay)

- PAGE International Screenwriting Awards
  (http://pageawards.com)

- Slamdance (www.slamdance.com)

The most important screenplay contest is the Nicholl Fellowships in Screenwriting. To make the semifinals, your script has to stay in the running from the 8,000 or more entries down to 152! If you place in the semifinals, expect email contact from agents, managers, and production companies. It's a very prestigious contest that is sponsored by the Academy Awards.

You could also enter local contests, which might have less prestige, but will also have fewer entries, increasing your chance of winning.

Beware of contests that promise the world — many times their claims about helping your career are exaggerated. Note that many of these contests have entry fees of $40 or more, so be choosy about which contests you enter.

In addition to the contests listed, there are some others that may be worth entering, depending on your genre and focus. MovieBytes.com offers an excellent overview of all the various competitions, along with scorecards and evaluations of each contest from screenwriters who have previously entered. It's a great way to help you evaluate which contests might be right for you.

My research into what kinds of scripts win these competitions have convinced me that independent-type, artsy stories are the ones that usually place well in these competitions. A great way to study what is winning is to read the winning scripts. The Nicholl Fellowships in Screenwriting lists on its website the screenplays which have won the competition, and also the ones which were made into movies. A few notable scripts that won the competitions and which were also produced include:

- *Akeelah and the Bee*

- *Down in the Delta*

- *Finding Forrester*

To purchase a copy of these winning scripts, you might try donedealpro.com or another script sales site.

I suggest you read and/or study the movies of these winning scripts to get a good idea of the types of scripts that win, and then write a story in a similar flavor. If you are serious about placing in one of the screenwriting competitions, you will have to write the type of screenplay that wins. Otherwise, you may be wasting your time. If you feel as though you might not ever be able to write the type of screenplay that wins, then this strategy might not be right for you.

3.4 Strategy 4: Work for, intern, or volunteer for an industry professional

If you live in Los Angeles, New York, Toronto, or Vancouver, a great way to make a connection and break into the industry is to work where the action is. Think about applying for a job, intern position, or volunteering with a literary agency or production company. While you're working there, you may want to form friendships as well. With friends on the inside, you won't be outside for long!

To find volunteer opportunities in the industry you could call production companies and managers listed in the *Hollywood Creative Directory*. Do a Google search for volunteer opportunities in the movie industry, or go to the following websites:

- Hollywood Film Festival and Hollywood Film Awards (www.hollywoodawards.com/volunteer.html)
- Film Crew Pro (www.filmcrewpro.com)
- Canadian Film Centre (www.cfccreates.com)
- National Screen Institute — Canada (www.nsi-canada.ca)

The heart and money of the movie industry is in Los Angeles. You may consider moving there, but it is a huge decision and one that shouldn't be made lightly. The cowriter of *Crash*, Bobby Moresco, sold his home and moved to Los Angeles. He got into the theater scene, and showcased his writing everywhere he could before connecting with Paul Haggis and writing *Crash*.

3.5 Strategy 5: Hire an agent

There are many ways to try to get your script made. One of the most conventional is to find an agent. Agents are important because they are the conduit, the connection between you — being on the outside of the movie-making world — and the people who can change your life, those in power in the business. Agents are the go-betweens. They represent all above-the-line talent such as directors, actors, and writers. If you're looking for an agent, here's how to proceed:

- Read the trade magazines, online sources, and *Hollywood Creative Directory* and find agents who are selling spec (original or adapted) material. Find agents who are selling your genre.

- Write a query letter. As suggested in section **3.2**, tailor it to each agent, and make it tight. Don't forget to enclose a self-addressed stamped envelope.

- Wait for a response. If the agent rejects you, don't sweat it, just move on.

- If the agent asks to see your script, he or she will ask you to sign a release form. Sign it, and send it along with your script.

- Wait for a response. If the agent rejects your script, don't give up; instead, plot your next move.

- If you get interest, the agent will contact you via phone or email. He or she will want to meet if he or she is interested in representing you.

- At the meeting with the agent, ask lots of questions.

- If you get a good vibe, sign with the agent. The contract should be for a period of no more than two years. The agent should get either 10 or 15 percent, no more. At this stage, you might want to get an entertainment lawyer to look over the paperwork.

Agents will send you out for "assignment" work on movies being made. They'll show your script around to potential producers for possible funding, but also as a writing sample for you as a writer on another project. This is how most writers in the Writers Guild of America (WGA) make their living. Thus, agents are a critical part of the process.

You sign a contract with an agent for an agreed-upon amount of time, often two years. This is why it's important to ask questions when you first meet. You want to make sure you can work with this person. What's the expression? Be careful who you get into bed with.

If the agent relationship isn't working, it's usually more of a mutual decision to split up. For example, the agent may feel that you're not bringing in enough money to justify the time he or she spends on you. Or, you may feel the agent is not spending enough time to get your script out there and get some action on it. There are two sides to every coin. Bottom line: If you're ready to move on from an agency, *don't* burn bridges. Word gets around town quickly. You don't want to be blacklisted from your next opportunity.

Agents are in extreme demand. You don't "hire" an agent. They take you on, if you're lucky enough. To get an agent is extremely difficult, but it can happen. For example, the coauthor of this book, Paul Peditto, used a query letter to get an agent with the William Morris Agency.

3.6 Strategy 6: Hire an entertainment attorney

Although many entertainment attorneys do not consider submitting screenplays to production companies and studios to be legal work, with a little research and a little luck, you might land one who will do that for you.

Please note that entertainment attorneys usually do not work on commission like agents and managers. They are paid up front whether they sell your screenplay or not. If you should decide to invest in one, you will be expected to pay a retainer fee, starting at $1,500, and you will be billed hourly: roughly $200, $300, or maybe even $400 an hour for his or her services. However, if your attorney can get your script in the right hands, it might be worth it.

You want an entertainment lawyer when you get a bite; when someone notices your script and wants to be in business with you. When paperwork needs to be drawn up, you need a lawyer.

To locate entertainment attorneys, subscribe to *Hollywood Creative Directory* for an extensive listing. Lawyers for the Creative Arts (www.law-arts.org) offers free or low-budget entertainment law services. Entertainment attorneys are just as selective as agents and managers. Some of them will be interested in your story and others will not.

3.7 Strategy 7: Attend a class

Consider enrolling in a class taught by an industry professional, be it acting, directing, or writing. If the instructor is an industry professional, it's a great way for you to get to know him or her as a friend or contact. One notable screenwriter was able to secure a deal with Sony Pictures by meeting an associate in a screenwriting class! Not only is it an excellent way to learn a new skill, it's a great way for an industry professional to get to know you.

Enrolling in film school can be a huge expense (e.g., Columbia College costs $20,000 a year). However, there are great adult education opportunities that cost considerably less. Mediabistro (www.mediabistro.com/courses) offers reasonably priced classes online. You can also find some great courses at New York Film Academy (www.nyfa.edu). The UCLA School of Theater, Film, and Television (www.tft.ucla.edu) has an incredible online resource called UCLA extension (www.uclaextension.edu) that has Writers Guild of America (WGA) accredited writers teaching classes online. Vancouver Film School (VFS) is another well-known institution (www.vfs.com).

Of course, online courses won't necessarily help you connect with others to sell your script. However, improving your writing and learning about the industry through these courses will point you in the right direction. If you physically go to classes, you may have a professor or classmates who can put you in touch with others in the industry. Once again, it comes down to relationships and who you know in the industry.

3.8 Strategy 8: Attend pitch seminars

A great way to market your script is to attend a pitch seminar and pitch your story up close and in person, directly to an industry professional. The Screenwriting Expo (www.screenwritingexpo.com) is just such an event, which is held annually in Los Angeles in the fall.

There is learning to be had from major industry professionals who congregate at pitch seminars, but don't be a stalker. Industry professionals are besieged with desperate writers looking to pitch their script so don't be "that guy"! Go to the pitch seminars to expand your knowledge of the business and craft of screenwriting.

3.9 Strategy 9: Self-publish your screenplay

Self-publishing is no new phenomenon to the novelist or the nonfiction writer; however, to the aspiring screenwriter, it is an untapped market with huge prospects. Self-publishing your screenplay will offer you an alternative approach to breaking into the industry.

There are online websites such as Talentville, InkTip, and Trigger Street Labs where you can, without an agent, upload your script for viewing and critique. It's a nice option for those without agents; a long shot, as far as actually getting a movie made, but for you to get noticed, it may be worth it.

4. Summarize Your Screenplay

Since time is precious in the movie world, you may be asked to give a logline, synopsis, and/or a screen treatment. These are short descriptions of your overall story. You want to sell your work, so make sure you get your story's description across in an interesting way with the fewest words.

4.1 Logline and synopsis

When someone asks you about your script, inevitably the person will ask for a *logline* and a *synopsis*. The reason? The two together can be read in about a minute. Remember, time is precious, so take the time to write a great logline and synopsis.

Samples 4 and 5 were written by Paul Peditto. Sample 4 is about a black comedy called *Skin Deep*, which made it to the quarterfinal round at the Nicholl Fellowships for Screenwriters.

Sample 5 is a synopsis for a drama called *The 16th Minute*. Notice the change in tone from the previous sample. Sample 5 is not written for comedy, so the logline and synopsis reflect that.

4.2 Screenplay treatment

The screenplay treatment is a description of the style of the story and how you will unfold the narrative. It is used to convince the reader that there is a story and that you can tell the story well. It is basically a synopsis of the story without the minute details (i.e., setting, dialogue, and location); instead it is an overall view of the story.

SAMPLE 4
Logline and Synopsis: *Skin Deep*

SKIN DEEP

LOGLINE:
After an accident, a lifelong nerd is remade, with plastic surgery, into a hunk. Finding the girl of his high-school obsession 25 years later, he ends up with her 21-year-old daughter, with bloody results.

SYNOPSIS:
Jeff Dale, high-school loser, has one obsession: Abby Goodman, cheerleading queen. Alas, Abby is together with Chase Carson, football captain and god. To be close to her, Jeff becomes the team mascot. Life is pretty much pathetic.

Flash forward 25 years. After a traffic accident, Jeff meets Dr. Sunblade, the Picasso of plastic surgeons. An experimental technique transforms Jeff — the geek is reborn.

At their 25th high school reunion, Jeff finds Abby married to her football god, Chase. Their glory days are over. When Abby throws herself at Jeff, the fantasy doesn't measure up. Instead, a new fantasy presents itself: Tara, her 21-year-old daughter. It leads to them hooking up, and Abby going Mrs. Robinson on her daughter. Hubby Chase ends up dead and Tara barely escapes with her life. When Jeff plays white knight and steals away with Tara, Abby and her personal trainer, Cecil, track them down, culminating in a neo-noir nightmare of Botox dosing, bubbling liquefied fat, and gun-crazy danger.

SAMPLE 5
Logline and Synopsis: *The 16th Minute*

THE 16th MINUTE

LOGLINE:
A reclusive Nobel Prize-winning scientist stalks a famous Talk TV hostess to avenge the death of his daughter.

SYNOPSIS:
With her ratings in the toilet, Susanne Dare, Talk TV goddess, pushes a young guest too far. When the guest kills herself, her father — reclusive, Nobel Prize-winning scientist Dr. Steven Kemp — begins to stalk Susanne. Kemp becomes "the Nobel Savage," a tabloid sensation. The 24/7 media monster that Susanne once fed now feeds on her. Dr. Kemp, the smartest guy in any room, evades police until Susanne presents him with an offer he can't refuse: Kill her on live, national TV. Part-thriller, part-drama, part-satire. *Network* for the reality TV age.

If you know your story well, the treatment will not be too difficult to write. However, if you are still flushing out the story, you may find it difficult to write the treatment.

A treatment is sometimes written in advance of writing the script. A producer will ask to read the smallest amount possible to get a sense of the story, so this is where a treatment would come in handy. Treatments are in prose paragraph form, written in third person, present tense, with observable behavior and limited dialogue.

The treatment is usually 10 to 20 pages long. It's usually about a page of treatment for ten pages of script. Thus, a 10- or 15-page treatment is just about right for a feature-length script. (See Sample 6.)

SAMPLE 6
Screenplay Treatment

An irresistible attorney struggles to find true love but only seems capable of attracting sex-starved women.

Spring in Chicago. It's raining cats, dogs, and donkeys.

It's two o'clock in the morning when KANDY CLARK (29), a petite sex kitten, arrives at the apartment of Josh John and Billie Ray. JOSH JOHN (30) is a red-haired skeptic, attractive in an unusual sort of way. BILLIE RAY (28) is a lipstick lesbian who rides a motorcycle. Three times a week, Kandy makes her routine visits to Josh's apartment with one goal in mind — to get her freak on.

Wanting more than just a sexual relationship, Josh makes his 19th attempt to break off the relationship, but Kandy wants what she wants and she's not taking no for an answer. Climbing on Josh's back, Kandy convinces him that things will be different this time; she even promises to attend a film festival with him. Immediately after Kandy has her way with Josh, she dresses quickly, despite Josh's insistence that she stay the night. Kandy's comment: "We don't have that kind of relationship."

We are introduced to Josh's psychologist, DR. ARNIE BERRY (60) who is the epitome of Mr. Magoo. Dr. Berry is a bona fide nut who misconstrues everything Josh says.

Covered in despair and shame, Josh confesses to Dr. Berry that he succumbed to temptation again with Kandy. However, Dr. Berry seems more concerned with whether or not Josh hears voices.

A day later, Kandy reneges on her promise to attend the film festival with Josh, and she even refuses to have dinner with him. Her reasoning: She's too busy.

While flying back from the film festival, a woman literally falls into Josh's lap. She is KEMBER CLARK (29), a pretty intellect with designer glasses. They soon realize that they work for the same firm yet have never met. Right away, sparks fly between the two.

We learn more about his roommate, Billie, when Josh arrives home to a lipstick-lesbian movie club.

Excalibur Nightclub — a crowded office party. This place is swarming with impersonators: Marilyn Monroe, Elvis, Diana Ross, and Pee-Wee Herman.

We meet Josh's friend and colleague, ROB SAMUELS (31), who looks like a male escort. Though Rob is very much in love with his girlfriend, he is terrified of marriage, and he doesn't keep his opinion to himself.

At the bar, Josh is constantly hit on by secretaries, even other attorneys. Enter RITA MOORE (27), a scrumptious sex goddess who is determined to take Josh home with her. Rita convinces Josh to join her at the palm reader's booth so that they can have their futures revealed. Reluctantly, Josh agrees and learns that the love of his life will possess the initials KC.

At an outdoor café, Josh shares with his roommate, Billie, his disbelief that someone with the initials KC is out there waiting for him. For the first time, we learn that Dr. Berry is Billie's uncle and that as a favor to Billie, Josh has agreed to meet with him to restore Dr. Berry's confidence after having his license suspended. During lunch, we meet WILMA MAZA (36), who dresses like she's 60 and has the major hots for Josh. She makes no secret of her wishes to bear Josh's children.

Josh and his roommate, Billie, arrive home to a waiting Kandy, dressed in a French maid's uniform. She has yet to accept the dissolution of their sexual relationship. "Just one more time," she says, but Josh is not giving in to her.

When Josh questions Billie about the beautiful women she entertained at her movie party, Billie insists that her life is perfect the way it is and would rather not alter it with a relationship.

Josh is informed that he will have a temporary secretary in the absence of his regular secretary. He is pleasantly surprised to learn that it is Kember Clark — as in KC, possibly the love of his life.

Believing that Kember is "the one," Josh watches her from a distance, admiration in his eyes as he studies her every move.

Kandy arrives at Josh's office, makes one last attempt to rekindle their sexual fling, but Josh has made up his mind, and he's not backing down.

Josh's friend Rob insists that he and his girlfriend have the makings of a wonderful relationship, if only she would forget about marriage. Josh shares with Rob that he and Billie used to be an item and since then they have become the best of friends.

Dr. Berry's office — Josh shares with Dr. Berry his attraction and affections toward Kember. Dr. Berry is only concerned with whether Josh thinks of killing himself.

Josh wants to learn as much about Kember as he can before asking her out. He finds out that she's into Pilates and that one of her favorite books is *Beloved*.

Josh invites Kember to lunch to thank her for all the work she's done, except he hasn't given her any work to do. During lunch, Josh learns that he and Kember have a lot in common, including a love for reggae music. Josh invites himself to her Pilates class.

Josh asks Billie to read *Beloved* and write him a detailed outline so that he can comment on the book to Kember. He would rather not read it himself. When Billie says no, he has no choice but to turn to someone he knows will do anything for him: Wilma. Wilma agrees to write him a detailed summary of the novel provided he go out with her. Reluctantly, Josh agrees. When Josh tries to discuss *Beloved* with Kember, he soon learns that Kember never read the book.

Josh attempts to get Billie to start dating again, but Billie is convinced that being single is better than chancing a broken heart.

Josh attends Kember's Pilates class and makes a spectacle of himself, being the only male in the class. Afterwards, Josh expresses his feelings for Kember, but she is reluctant to date someone she works for. If she didn't work for him, things might be different.

Josh discusses with Dr. Berry Kember's reluctance to date him. Dr. Berry's advice: Fire her.

Josh is doubtful that Kember and he will ever become a couple, but his roommate, Billie, is sure of it, so much that she offers him some advice: "No matter how much she may want to, don't have sex with her."

Determined not to be manipulated, Josh's friend Rob is certain that his girlfriend is studying the book *The Rules* in order to learn how to nab a husband. So, as to deflect anything his girlfriend may have planned for him, he studies the book himself.

At a grocery store, we are introduced to REAGAN BUSH (27) a giggly woman from Josh's past who is determined to win him back. She even attempts to seduce him in the grocery store, but Josh remains strong.

Josh confides to his friend, Rob, that he feels as though he is swarming in women and can't get out, except for the one woman he wants, but can't have.

Wilma shows up at Josh's apartment to collect on their deal. Though Josh offers to take her to dinner and a movie, Wilma would rather he make love to her until she passes out. She's disappointed when he does not oblige.

Josh makes another attempt to convince Kember to date him by dictating a letter to her, stating how perfect they are for each other. Kember is impressed, but she does not change her mind.

Desperate to win Kember's heart, Josh secretly has Kember reassigned so that she no longer works for him. Kember is outraged when she learns of this, even threatens to bite off Josh's nose. Covering his nose, Josh denies having anything to do with it, but she doesn't buy it.

Josh's friend, Rob, convinces Kember that Josh had nothing to do with her reassignment, and she believes him even though Josh lied about the whole thing.

Kember shows up at Josh's apartment and apologizes for her accusations. Just when their relationship is about to begin, Kember and Billie hit it off when Kember learns that Billie rides a motorcycle. This connection of theirs does not rest well with Josh. He comments to Billie, "Don't try any funny stuff and you bring her right back."

"The woman of my dreams ran off with a lesbian," Josh says to Rob the next day. Although Rob assures him that Kember is not a lesbian, Josh is doubtful.

We are introduced to TRIXIE RICHARDS (27), chesty and full of life. She approaches Josh on the street, wanting very badly to ignite what could have been, but Josh remains strong.

At an elegant restaurant, Josh, Kember, Rob, and his girlfriend have dinner. Rob's girlfriend, HELEN GREEN (36) has the face of gloom. When Rob shares his pessimistic views of marriage again, Helen suggests that he remain single forever.

Upon arriving home, a bouquet of flowers awaits Billie, and Josh is certain they are from Kember. His concern is put to rest when he learns otherwise. Billie reassures him that Kember is not gay. Now Josh can breathe easily. He's happy that Billie has broken out of her shell and ventured out into the world of romance.

Rob is in mourning when Helen breaks off their relationship because of his critical beliefs about marriage.

Josh and Kember's relationship thrives. They share movies, midnight drives, massages, reggae concerts, even their own song: "Is This Love?"

When the big moment arrives for Josh and Kember to make love, Josh is hesitant for fear that she may be just like all the rest.

At Dr. Berry's office, Josh concludes that there is nothing wrong with him. He just needed to meet the right woman. "That's a matter of opinion," Dr. Berry says. Dr. Berry suggests to Josh that until he consummates the relationship, he will never know for sure if Kember is the one.

Josh and Kember arrange to have a long romantic lunch at his apartment, but their plans are halted when Josh is called to a last-minute meeting.

The next day, the big moment arrives, and Josh and Kember finally make love. To Josh's surprise, Kember has to leave immediately afterwards. Josh's jaw drops, it's happening all over again.

The next day Josh suggests he and Kember have dinner, but Kember is unavailable for the rest of the week.

Josh sings the blues to Dr. Berry: "Kember is just like all the rest." His dream of connecting with that special someone was just a fantasy.

Billie suggests that Josh allow Kember to explain her actions before giving up so soon.

Kember shows up at Josh's apartment with a gift: A Bob Marley CD box set. She was genuinely busy with work the previous week and also helping her sister through a devastating breakup.

Because it sounds too good to be true, Josh is convinced that he's on some hidden camera show, but soon he realizes otherwise.

Billie introduces Josh to her new girlfriend and informs him that she will not be home for dinner.

Josh and Kember are so captivated with each other that they attempt to outdo each other with compliments.

At the height of their relationship, Josh learns that Kember is the sister of Kandy, the woman he had meaningless sex with for several months. Embarrassed and ashamed, Josh breaks off the relationship and totally avoids Kember.

Rob's ex-girlfriend, Helen, gives Rob a second chance and Rob is a different man.

In Josh's heart, he knows he and Kember belong together and despite his shady history, he makes a stand for love and Kember, and even hires a Bob Marley impersonator to perform their favorite song.

A DOUBLE WEDDING: Josh and Kember and Rob and Helen. Rob's last words: "She made me do it."

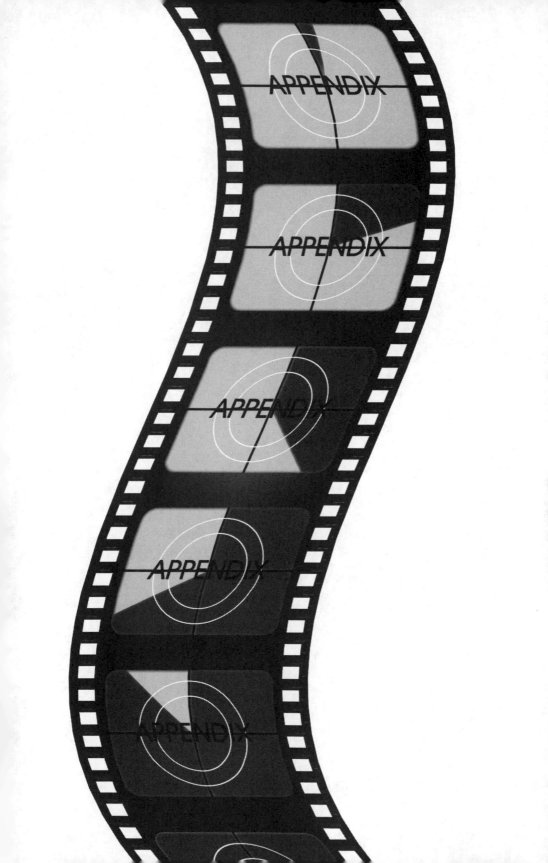

Appendix
Pictures of Baby Jane Doe

by Paul Peditto

1 EXT. HIGHWAY MEDIAN- ATLANTIC CITY- SUMMER DAY

A MAN in his 20's stands in the middle of a four lane highway.
He holds a pink toy duck. Cars pass, HORNS blast, drivers
CURSE him, but he doesn't hear. This is HORACE. In VOICE OVER,
we HEAR:

>   HORACE(V.O.)
> When I was three I was run over by a car.
> I mean run <u>over</u>. The tires missed my
> body by a few inches. I was dragged
> down the street by the muffler of a
> sixteen year old girl with her learner's
> permit. She was learning allright, and
> so was I.

2 EXT. BOARDWALK- DAY- MOMENTS EARLIER

HORACE walking at us. Atlantic City in the distance. 13
casinos shine on a flat horizon. OVER:

>   HORACE(V.O.)
> Later I was told about the screams of
> neighbors, the screams of my mother,
> a two hundred pound man lifting the two
> ton car to free me. You hear stories
> like that on the news. You never think
> it can happen to you.

3 EXT. STREET- NEW YORK CITY- DAY- SIX MONTHS EARLIER

A YOUNG WOMAN running at us. OVER:

>   HORACE(V.O.)
> My mother said there was no change in me
> after that. If only she knew. For on
> that day I developed a new appreciation
> for the inevitability of events. Sure,
> I was three, but I could see it all
> before me. Call it what you want. Luck.
> Fate. Forces old as time. Drawing us
> together. It was a fixed game played out
> ten times ten thousand times before.
> Only never to me.

The WOMAN closer. Crooked heels. Cheap Jack skirt and
sunglasses. Closer. Wild hair. Hollywood smile. Flying
toward us like a vision, and the FILM flashing to WHITE...

TITLE and CREDITS roll.

4   INT. HORACE'S ROOM- HOTEL RIVERVIEW- NEW YORK- DAY

An impossibly small, absolutely laughable prison cell of a
room. HORACE, in Hawaiian t-shirt and baggy pants, hits a
typewriter, pulling out paper and sticking it up against a
wall collage of scribbled writings, crime photos by Weegie,
obscure miscellania. OVER:

>   HORACE(V.O.)
>   It was spring time in New York. I took
>   another job that week bartending in a
>   transvestite nightclub. I measured it
>   up against the other jobs I'd held that
>   month: Vibrating pillow salesman. Horse
>   and carriage driver. Dishwasher.

Laying on the bed, HORACE cracks open a fortune cookie,
reading his fortune, tossing it in a bin of hundreds of
fortunes. OVER:

>   HORACE(V.O.)
>   It was fine.

5   EXT. STREET- MEATMARKET DISTRICT- DAY

A MAN WITH A MATTRESS tied to his back pisses against a
building, a stream forms under him. OVER:

>   HORACE(V.O.)
>   I was lucky to find the work.

HORACE walks through the puddle of piss without noticing,
through the door of a hole-in-the-wall club.

6   INT. ENCHILADA CLUB- DAY- LATER

Two catatonic TRANSVESTITES slow dance under a mini-disco ball
in purple limelight.

Two other TRANSVESTITES sit at the bar, TRANSVESTITE 1 dabs
at a cut on TRANSVESTIVE 2's forehead, pointing to HORACE
who digs inside a large jar of pickled pig's feet.

>   TRANSVESTITE 1
>   Not that one!

                    HORACE
         They're all the same.

                    TRANSVESTITE 1
         Excuse me! I am the customer! The
         customer is always right, honey! That
         one. With the small toes. I'm on a
         diet.

THE FRONT DOOR bursts open. The YOUNG WOMAN we saw running
enters fast, past the dancing TRANSVESTITES, to the bar.
Stamp tattoos on her back and shoulder read: "HANDLE WITH CARE"
and "URGENT". This is JANE.

                    JANE
         Oh, I'm out of breath! I need
         something. Whatcha got, Budweiser?
         Hon'? What?

HORACE is staring at the tattoos.

                    HORACE
         Nothing.

                    JANE
         You got the tall boys or the regular?
         Or the ponies? The little ones. They
         go down better. Easier. Ok gimme a
         regular.
                    (HORACE MOVES FOR IT)
         No, wait!
                    (HORACE STOPS)
         A tall boy, big boy! With a straw!
         Can't get it down without one!

HORACE goes for beer, JANE sees TRANSVESTITE 2's cut.

                    JANE
         Honey, what happened to you?

                    TRANSVESTITE 1
         She had a little fall.

                    TRANSVESTITE 2
                    (wasted)
         I'm gonna be scarred!

Looking her over:

                    JANE
         No you won't. It's just a cut. It'll
         heal in two days.

                    TRANSVESTITE 1
          How do you know?

                    JANE
          Honey, I'm an expert on the subject.

Removes the sunglasses to show her eye: Ugly purple, badly
smashed.

                    TRANSVESTITE 1
          What happened?

                    JANE
          You don't wanna know.

                    TRANSVESTITE 1
          I smell a man's hand.

                    JANE
          Try two. Men that is. Four hands.
                    (HORACE RETURNS WITH BEER & STRAW)
          Thanks, darlin'. I like your shirt. I
          love Hawaiians.

                    TRANSVESTITE 1
          Men are such Nazis.

The TRANSVESTITES look hard to HORACE, who is confused as to
why.

                    JANE
          Nah, it's just me. I told you, I'm like
          a bad fruit. I'll bump into a mailbox,
          get a bruise that last weeks.

                    HORACE
          Bump into many mailboxes, do you?

                    JANE
          Yeah. I'm what you might call accident
          prone.

Putting sunglasses back on, with a smile at HORACE, which is
returned.

                    HORACE
          I got a little of that in me too.

Reaching for makeup:

                    TRANSVESTITE 1
          Try this.

ANGLE DANCEFLOOR, the MUSIC switches, the comatose TRANS-
VESTITES dance unchanged, holding each other up in purple neon.

                    JANE(O.S.)
          No, thanks. I've powdered this eye in every
          bathroom in the city the last two days. I
          got the story down. Anyone asks, I'll tell
          'em I'm a lady wrestler. They gimme any
          backtalk, I'll give 'em a bodyslam!

ANGLE BAR, JANE gives a headlock and knuckle grind demonstration,
HORACE laughing. Flirting:

                    HORACE
          So how did you get that eye?

Coyly sipping Bud from a straw, like a schoolgirl:

                    JANE
          I told you. A mailbox.

                    HORACE
          It doesn't look bad.

                    JANE
          Oh sure. I get lots of compliments on
          this side of my face.

                    HORACE
          You look good.

ANGLE TRANSVESTITES, a look to each other and groan, watching
HORACE move closer, the come on.

                    JANE
          Honey, please, I'm falling to pieces,
          let's face it, I'm falling to pieces.
          My nose needs pinching, my jaw's outta
          whack with the rest of my face, now my
          eye--

                    HORACE
          You look good.

                    JANE
          Yeah?

                    HORACE
          Yeah.

                    JANE
          Well, darlin'...

CONTINUED:

Lowering the shades with a smile:

                    JANE(CONT.)
          ...Tell me more.

FREEZE FRAME. JANE'S face. OVER:

                    HORACE(V.O.)
          What she saw in me I really don't know.
          Maybe it was mind.

7   EXT. DOORWAYS- MEATMARKET DISTRICT- NIGHT

WILD MUSIC UP. JANE and HORACE in and out of doorways,
kissing, all over each other. HORACE trying to save it
for later but JANE ready now.

8   INT. HORACE'S ROOM- HOTEL RIVERVIEW- NIGHT- LATER

The laughably small room now fits two, JANE atop HORACE in bed,
kissing his chest, working her way down.

                    JANE
               (slurring, as if drunk)
          Here?

JANE spacy. Kissing lower.

                    JANE
          Here.

HORACE about to explode, then not, looking up to find JANE
passed out on his stomach. Looking to his wall collage.

CLOSE ON TWO PHOTOS, two laughing women with stamp tattoos
exactly as JANE'S: "HANDLE WITH CARE"--"URGENT".

BACK TO HORACE, considering coincidence, fate, letting
JANE sleep, a crooked beauty about her.

9   INT. HORACE'S ROOM- NIGHT- HOURS LATER

DARKNESS. JANE wakes, waking HORACE. A match struck, a
candle lit. JANE looking for something.

                    JANE
          Hey, that was great. Really. Really
          great.

                    HORACE
          You passed out.

                    JANE
          I didn't. Did I?

Horace shakes yes.

                    JANE
          God. No. Really? Jez. No sleep in
          two days, my brain goes to mush. I'm
          sorry. I been in a fog the last couple
          weeks. It's not you. I mean, I hope
          you don't think--

                    HORACE
          No, it's allright. I have that effect
          on women.

JANE finds what she was looking for, placing her sunglasses
on, moving atop HORACE, blowing the candle out:

                    JANE
          Let's see who passes out this time.

10 INT. HORACE'S ROOM- NEXT MORNING

HORACE wakes. Alone. Looking around. Jane is gone.
Laying back in bed, a look of disappointment, when...

JANE opens the door, her bag in hand, a magazine of
HORACE'S in the other.

                    JANE
          I just took it to the bathroom. You
          read Evil Eye. I love that rag.
          Read it religiously.

Not sure why, but happy to see her, quietly:

                    HORACE
          I don't read it. I write it. I'm in
          there.

                    JANE
          You're a writer? I ain't nev-- I mean,
          I haven't ever met a writer before. What
          name you go under?

                    HORACE
          Ignatz Kelly.

JANE SCREAMS. HORACE jumps.

>   JANE
>   Holy shit! Ignatz Kelly! I read you!
>   Lots of times! Wow. Here I was with
>   a celebrity and not knowing it!

A ZOMBIE-LIKE MAN walks by the open doors, stops, walks by.

>   HORACE
>   Could you close the door.

>   JANE
>   I can't believe it. You're not
>   kiddin', right, you're really him.

HORACE sadly shakes yes.

>   JANE
>   I seen you in lots of rags. I read 'em
>   all. Hellbent. Amor Fati. New Crime
>   Stories. Ignatz Kelly!

>   HORACE
>   That's a psuedonym. It's not my real
>   name. I told you my name last night.

>   JANE
>   (embarrassed)
>   I forgot.

>   HORACE
>   Horace.

>   JANE
>   Horace. That's nice. Why doncha use
>   Horace?

>   HORACE
>   It's stupid.

>   JANE
>   It is not! It's got a ring to it. Better
>   than Jane. Plain Jane! That's me. Horace
>   has a ring to it. O'course, Ignatz does
>   too. Either way you're ok, I guess. Oh
>   well...

Putting his magazine down:

>   JANE
>   Better shove off. It sure was fun.

                    HORACE
          Where you going?

                    JANE
          The Dumpling House. Stanton and
          Rivington. My stuff's there. Can't
          leave it too long. You know the
          neighborhood.

                    HORACE
          You live there?

                    JANE
          Temporarily, Hon'. We'll see ya on
          down the line, right!

JANE out the door, HORACE barely able to react:

                    HORACE
          Wait a minute...Hey! Wanna make 20 bucks!?

JANE reappears in the doorway, making a face.

                    JANE
          You're supposed to ask me that
          before, Hon'.

                    HORACE
          I'm serious.

                    JANE
          Doin' what? Nothing too weird.

HORACE just smiles, as we:

CUT TO:
11   INT. BATHROOM- HOTEL RIVERVIEW- DAY

RAPID FIRE LIGHT BULBS FLASH, one, two, three...we see JANE
dead...sprawled, contorted in a tub, her head badly bloodied
when... her hand moves, up, to scratch her nose.

                    HORACE(O.S.)
          Don't move!

HORACE moves to the tub, around his neck is an old style
Kodak with Graflex flash, touching up JANE'S death makeup.

                    JANE
          Sorry.

                    HORACE
          This is specific. She's gotta look
          an exact way. Don't move.

Solemnly:

                    JANE
          Got it. Who am I, again?

HORACE backs off. More old time light bulb FLASHES.

                    HORACE
          Diavala. Barnum and Bailey high diver.
          Routinely diving from a 200 foot ladder
          into a six foot canvas tank. One day,
          while bathing, she slips on a cake of
          soap. Falling. Smashing her skull
          against the edge of the tub. A piquant
          tragedy.

12 INT. BATHROOM- DAY- LATER

HORACE and JANE take a break, eating lunch. JANE eats fast,
devouring the meal as if it's her first in days, talking all
the while. HORACE just watches her.

                    JANE
          ...weird dreams! I had one. I was
          shoplifting a can of green beans and a
          stockboy caught me. I made a run for it
          and hid behind this Cheez Whiz display.
          But he saw me and jumped in his zamboni,
          that cleaning machine. He was coming
          down the aisle around 40 miles an hour,
          about to run me over when I woke up.
          That's all I remember. Cheez Whiz.
          You get weird dreams?

Caught up watching her, shaking no:

                    HORACE
          I get the same dream every night.

Chomping her food:

                    JANE
          Aha.

                    HORACE
          A blonde eating a peach in the Pompeii ruins.

Considering this:

                    JANE
          Pompeii, huh.
                    (pause&thinking)
          So how come you wanted me for the photos?

                        HORACE
            Pictures accompany the story. Professional
            models cost 200 an hour.

                        JANE
            Not me, Hon'! I come cheap. I haven't
            worked in years. I try, y'know, I really
            do, but it never works out. I shoulda
            taken computer class like my Dad said.
            You gotta have training.

Watching her wolf the food down, offering the remainder of
his food, which she takes and eats.

                        JANE
            Can I ask ya something? I wasn't gonna,
            but... how come you work in that bar?
            You're a great writer, you do the photos
            'n all--

                        HORACE
            They don't pay.

                        JANE
            Some pay. I read it somewhere. This one
            article, it said most writers are geniuses.
            They got big brain development. Bigger
            than most anyways. This one writer got
            scientists to pay him to will his brain
            to 'em after he died! Tell me that
            ain't brain power!

                        HORACE
            That's the dumbest thing I've ever heard.

                        JANE
            I'm tellin' you! Writers got big
            development.

Both thinking sex at once, big smiles.

                        JANE
            Brains!

13   INT. HALLWAY- DAY- LATER

HORACE and JANE walking down a nightmarish corridor. A neighbor,
RUDY, looks out as they pass, wearing an old bandstand cap
of moldy colored-feathers, watching HORACE and JANE in
amusement.

                    JANE
          So howja get your scars?

                    HORACE
          I got run over by a car. The wheels
          went on either side.
                    (demonstrates)
          If they'd gone like this...

14 INT. LOBBY- DAY

HORACE and JANE walk by, decorated in awful yellow checkerboard
wallpaper, an ELEVATOR BOY waits in a cubbyhole elevator and the
HOTEL MANAGER watching TV behind a steel reinforced cage.

                    JANE
          OhmyGod!

                    HORACE
          Pancake.

15 EXT. HOTEL RIVERVIEW- DAY

HORACE and JANE walk out on the street, the neighborhood
anything but romantic. The hotel is red brick. Outmoded
and oversized. WHORES walk the corners. The frozen Hudson
River beyond.

                    JANE
          You're lucky to be alive!

                    HORACE
          That's a matter of opinion.

16 EXT. MEATMARKETS- DAY

HORACE and JANE stopping outside a meat packaging plant.

                    JANE
          How can you joke like that?

                    HORACE
          Who's joking?

JANE taken aback at HORACE'S worldview. HORACE looking in...

P.O.V, EXTREME CLOSE UPS, MEAT WORKERS grinding leftover fat
and beef intestines through a huge vacuum. The SOUND and stench
of death overhelming.

BACK TO JANE looking in, smiling...

JANE'S P.O.V, an ITALIAN MAN sitting on a stool listens to
a radio nearly, the SOUND of OPERA rising up, joyfully.

JANE taking HORACE'S hand as they walk away. OVER:

>   HORACE(V.O.)
>   Fact being stranger than fiction sometimes,
>   I asked Jane to live with me, and she
>   agreed. I didn't know a thing about her.

17 EXT. THE DUMPLING HOUSE- STANTON & RIVINGTON- LATER

A burnt out building. A razed sign says: "Ho's Dumplings".
JANE and HORACE outside the building, looking up, waiting.
HORACE freaked by the surroundings but JANE all smiles,
kissing him as...

A jumbo garbage bag drops with a CRASH at their feet, tossed
from above. JANE looks up...

ANGLE THIRD STORY WINDOW, a woman, LUCINDA, looks down. JANE
picks up the bag, all her worldly possessions.

>   JANE
>   It's all here, right!?
>   (LUCINDA SHAKES YES)
>   I'm at the Lombard! C'mon by!

LUCINDA with a small smile and little interest, closing the
window.

ANGLE BELOW, HORACE picks up the garbage bag, looking to JANE,
wondering what the hell he's gotten himself into.

18 EXT. AMPITHEATER- DAY- LATER

HORACE and JANE walking back to the hotel with the garbage bag,
passing another burnt out building, JANE pulling HORACE inside.

19 INT. AMPITHEATER- SAME

CAMERA TRACKING behind them, this in the style of a Roman-style
ampitheater. JANE leading HORACE to a stage overlooking graffiti
and haunting, otherwordly ruins.

>   JANE
>   Bring on the lions, huh.

Looking out on the stark psuedo-Roman ruins:

```
                    HORACE
          Know what the Romans did?  In peacetime
          they filled the Coliseum up with water
          and recreated live naval battles.  War
          all the time.
```

19   INT. H & J'S ROOM- LATE NIGHT/3 A.M.- HORACE AND JANE

Looking upwards, wide awake and side by side in the tiny bed.
MUSIC beats in from the next room, MUMMERS STRING BAND MUSIC,
roaring in from RUDY'S, and his VOICE:

```
                    RUDY(O.S.)
          YOU LITTLE FUCKING BASTARD!
```

MUSIC and RANTS out. A pause. JANE happily holding HORACE.

```
                    JANE
          So what's that smell?  It's up here, in
          the lobby...
```

Nearly speechless with anger and sleeplessness:

```
                    HORACE
          Calves brains.

                    JANE
          Really?

                    HORACE
          The factory.  Calves brains, tongues.
          Beef tripe.  Scald 'em and sell 'em.

                    JANE
          God.
                    (pause)
          I thought tripe was fish.

                    HORACE
          It's beef.
```

SOUND of a RECORD SCRATCHING violently, more MUSIC, and
RUDY'S VOICE:

```
                    RUDY(O.S.)
          I DON'T GIVE A FITTING FUCK!  I'M
          EMULFINATING!  I'M SHRIEKING!
```

Up fast:

```
                    HORACE
          THAT'S IT!
```

                    JANE
          Easy, Hon'! He don't know any better--

HORACE moving for RUDY'S room, stopping, reaching for toilet
paper instead, stuffing his ears with it.

                    HORACE
          He used to knock off at 12, now he
          goes strong 'til 3! Rudy! Hal! You
          haven't heard Hal yet. He told me
          these rooms are smaller than his cell at
          Attica. Another man of culture!

                    JANE
          What're ya doin'?

                    HORACE
          Dialing out.

                    JANE
          Don't dial me out!

                    HORACE
          I gotta get some sleep, Jane!

                    JANE
          I'll put a spell on him...

Pulling HORACE back to bed, holding him close:

                    JANE
          I told you I was a witch, right? I like
          the white magic. Too many weird things
          goin' on with the black magic. I use it
          to ward off the evil eye, all that. I
          put a spell on you.

                    HORACE
          So lay one on Rudy.

                    JANE
          First thing in the morning.

Both looking up, seeing almost together...

ANGLE ON THE WALL, a cockroach crawls slowly upward.

                    HORACE
          I'll get it.

                    JANE
          No! Killing a small defenseless
          creature!?

HORACE frowns, moving to crush it.

                    JANE
    No!

                  HORACE
    I knew this guy. Compulsive gambler.
    We'd go down Atlantic City together.
    He bet me once which way a cockroach
    would crawl.

                    JANE
    I don't wanna take your money, honey.
    He's goin' left. I got animal instinct.

                  HORACE
    Oh yeah? What do you wanna bet?

                    JANE
    Loser wears diapers tomorrow night.

                  HORACE
    You are a kinky one, aren't ya.

CLOSE ON HORACE AND JANE, faces near the wall, rooting the
cockroach on.

                  HORACE
    C'MON, BABY!

                    JANE
    LEFT!

                  HORACE
    RIGHT ON RED! RIGHT!

The cockroach moves right.

                  HORACE
    YES!

HORACE and JANE back into bed laughing when... a KNOCK at the
door. JANE up to open the door.

RUDY is in the doorway, wearing bandstand cap and now, holding
his arms up high.

                  RUDY
    You're making a bloody racket!

Delighted to see him:

>   JANE
>   You're the man next door, right? Horace
>   told me about you. Rudy?

>   RUDY
>   I'm the arms-up man!
>   (JANE amazed)
>   I'll spend my life with my arms raised
>   in the air until everyone else does the
>   same, until everyone on the earth walks
>   with their arms high! Then I'll drop
>   mine.

Raising her arms high:

>   JANE
>   Well, it's a pleasure to meet you!

HORACE amazed at seeing RUDY at his door, and at JANE'S
reaction, up from bed as RUDY looks in.

>   RUDY
>   (to HORACE)
>   I had a friend who looked like you. He
>   cut off his penis and ran with it along
>   Interstate 80. He was a sad man.

HORACE is speechless, as we:

CUT TO:
20 EXT. PIER- DAY

JANE again contorted in a death pose, her neck twisted, her
limbs spread eagle upon a dilapidated pier. HORACE snaps off
photos, the bulbs FLASHING. OVER:

>   HORACE(O.S.)
>   Sally Wilson. Tight rope walker. Called
>   the Human Fly for her ability to defy
>   gravity. One day walking on a pier she
>   catches her toe in a plank and goes over,
>   head first, breaking her spine and neck
>   simultaniously. Causing instant death.

21 INT. H & J'S ROOM- DAY

JANE dead again, her head bloody and tongue out as bulbs POP
and FLASH. OVER:

> HORACE(O.S.)
> Mrs. Harvey Church. Killed by Mr. Church.
> His ordinary suburban home turned into a
> house of horror! His basement into a
> fiendish place! The matter-o-factness
> of his neighbors lives shattered forever!
> The crime reminding them a city street is
> not a city street, homey-looking houses
> are not homey-looking houses, that life,
> orderly, policed and conventionalized
> is nothing of the sort!

The BULBS stop popping and JANE opens her eyes, with a wink
and smile to HORACE.

22   EXT. HOTEL RIVERVIEW- DAY- LATER

CAMERA TRACKING with HORACE as the same beaten down WHORES
proposition him, HORACE just moving up the stairs...

22A INT. HALLWAY- HOTEL RIVERVIEW- SAME

CAMERA TRACKING with HORACE through the lobby of the Lombard,
into a claustrophobic elevator and out, through the hallway
straight up to his door before stopping, seeing it ajar and
HEARING, from within:

> RUDY(O.S.)
> I was in a 47th street strip house. An
> old man at the end of the bar fell out of
> his seat. He was watching a shining star
> on stage, a beautiful baby doll who didn't
> notice his fall or didn't care. I moved
> to help him up and the man turned and
> looked up at me with tears in his eyes.
> He was blind. Couldn't see a damn thing.
> It was then I decided to get out of New
> York.

HORACE opens the door, amazed to see...

JANE and RUDY on the bed, reading a blurb from his wall
collage.

> JANE
> Hey, Hon'! We were just reading some of
> your stuff. You don't mind, do ya?
> Whatja get, I'm starving!

Handing the bag to JANE with difficulty. Three in the tiny
room!-- Barely possible, the situation absurd.

Pulling out a Gerber's Vanilla Custard Pudding. Sticking
a finger in, licking:

                    JANE
          My favorite!

Closer to HORACE:

                    RUDY
                (meaning the wall blurb)
          Very poignant. Very noir.

                    JANE
          Rudy's a writer too!

                    RUDY
          Writing is disgusting. It's a secretion.
          Writers are a pack of cowardly, shit-scared
          gropers.

                    JANE
          He's suffering for his art!

In HORACE'S face, examining him:

                    RUDY
          He looks like dogshit.
                (to HORACE)
          I'd purchase a mirror. Look at yourself.
          Look at what you've become.

                    JANE
          Anyone for tea?

23 INT. H & J'S ROOM- DAY- MOMENTS LATER

Drinking tea and eating doughnuts:

                    JANE
          --Oh yeah! Things were looking mighty
          bleak 'til my honey came through, like
          the cavalry!

                    RUDY
          Into the valley of death rode the 600!

                    JANE
          Heroic!

                    RUDY
Heroic!
                (a rough eye on HORACE)
We have need of heroes now more than ever.

RUDY placing his doughnut down.

                    HORACE
I wouldn't do that. We've got bugs.

                    JANE
He's in all the latest 'zines! Hanging
Man 3. Beatniks From Space.

                    RUDY
A celebrity. Fascinated by Fate. There's
a raft of such cases one could remember.
Veteran barbers cutting themselves,
trapeze artists falling out of bed and
dying of injuries. North Pole explorers
freezing to death in a Philadelphia
basement. Why the fascination?

                    HORACE
I don't know.

                    RUDY
Recall the Norwegian proverb: "The life
of man is like the flight of a swallow
through a lighted feasting hall— out
of the dark, a brief moment of noise,
and back into the dark."

Tremendously impressed/considering this:

                    JANE
The flight of the swallow.

HORACE just looks to JANE, to RUDY, in disbelief. Looking
to RUDY'S doughnut...a big, juicy cockroach has jumped on,
making a meal of it!...HORACE just watches as RUDY picks
it back up to eat.

                    RUDY
Norwegians live the longest. Because of
pores. Not like in this city. You can't
breathe here. They keep the pores open
in Norway.

RUDY looking to the doughnut, to the cockroach, to HORACE,
a fearless smile, taking a huge bite!

24   INT. H & J'S ROOM- NIGHT

JANE dressing before a tiny mirror hung with fishing line.
HORACE upside down on the bed, in a headstand.

                    JANE
          I thought he made some good points.

                    HORACE
          The man is crazy, Jane.

                    JANE
          Y'gotta admit, Hon', you got some
          pretty weird shit on your walls.

                    HORACE
          Don't talk about my walls.

                    JANE
          And this room.

                    HORACE
          What about it?

                    JANE
          Nothing. But it's just a box.

Falling out of the headstand:

                    HORACE
          A box?

                    JANE
          Honey, don't get me wrong, I'm grateful.
          But with your brains--

                    HORACE
          Please, not the big brain theory again.
          I like my box. It protects me from the
          world. Most of the time.

Looking to JANE who sprays hairspray, teases hair, spraying on
on more in one motion, a whirl of activity, grimacing as she
brushes.

                    JANE
          You just gotta give people a chance.

Watching JANE, amazed/amused:

                    HORACE
          Looks like you got a few knots there.

                    JANE
          Feels like a robin's nest. I'm almost
          ready. How 'bout you?

                    HORACE
          I was ready an hour ago.

                    JANE
          Really? Not the jacket 'n tie type, huh.

Models earrings:

                    JANE
          You like these? Or these? Parrots! The
          next big thing. Hip, right? Got 'em for
          a buck on St. Mark's. They stole all my
          good jewelry at the Dumpling House. My
          tourqoise. A gold pinky ring. A ring of
          my mother's. I was sleepin' and they
          took it right off my finger.

                    HORACE
          Great friends you got.

                    JANE
          Uh uh.

JANE has taken her head in hands, one hand on her jaw, one
on her neck, twisting, cracking her neck.

                    HORACE
          Why do you do that?

                    JANE
          It relieves the tension, you goose.

                    HORACE
          Unbelievable.

                    JANE
          What unbelievable?

                    HORACE
          You unbelievable.

                    JANE
          Me unbelievable?

                    HORACE
          You unbelievable.

                    JANE
          I believe. You believe?

                    HORACE
          I believe.

                    JANE
          Stick with me, kid. I'll show you the
          world.

Putting on her shoes, they are hopelessly worn down at the
heel.

                    HORACE
          You oughta get to a heel bar.

                    JANE
          It's the way I walk. Pidgeontoed. Had
          it since birth. Terrible thing. Are
          you ready?

                    HORACE
                  (wearily)
          An hour ago.

JANE pulling out a bottle of Tylenol, taking out 4, sitting
and downing them one after another with tea, knocking the tea
down in a slug...HORACE watching as she looks up with a
Hollywood smile:

                    JANE
          Oh yeah! Let's go!

HORACE takes her hand, moving for the door.

                    JANE
          Wait! I didn't get...

Jamming blush, hairspray, Tylenol into her bag rapid fire,
taking HORACE'S her hand, almost out the door, when...

                    JANE
          Oh, wait!...

Moving for a large bottle of cheap perfume, tilting one side
against her neck, splashing, and repeating, turning to HORACE,
brightly beaming:

                    JANE
          Ready!

                        HORACE
            You're ready?

                        JANE
            Ready Freddy! How do I look? Up for
            Vogue or what!? Admit it, Hon', the kid
            looks like a star!

HORACE taking her hand and they go out the door.

25 EXT. CHINATOWN STREETS- NIGHT

HORACE and JANE on the town. Brights lights. Fiery Chinatown
landscape. Looking into shop window after shop window.

26 INT. CHINATOWN CLOTHING STORE- NIGHT- LATER

Checking out a rack of expensive clothes:

                        HORACE
            A hundred ten bucks?

                        JANE
            It's snakeskin! It doesn't grow on trees.

                        HORACE
            I saw some for twenty.

                        JANE
            Imitation, darling. See...

Checking out a rack of ties:

                        JANE
            Silkworm ties. 40 bucks each. The real
            deal.

                        HORACE
            Yeah, so?

Gleam in her eye, modeling one on HORACE, with an eye to the
SHOPKEEPER...

JANE'S P.O.V., the SHOPKEEPER turns a moment...

JANE quickly slipping a 40$ tie over HORACE'S neck...

                        HORACE
                        (laughing)
            What're you doing!? What're you--

                        JANE
                  (w/more meaning)
            Let's go.

A single look between them and HORACE realizes what she's
thinking, HORACE not wanting to and JANE looks at him square,
disappointed, HORACE with a smile and JANE smiling, HORACE
going with it and JANE beaming, kissing HORACE deep, breaking
away...

ANGLE JANE, moving toward the SHOPKEEPER, when...

WHAM!

She falls! Knocking over a huge rack of shirts, pants...

                        JANE
            AHHHHHHHH!

The SHOPKEEPER moving to her at once, helping her up.

                        JANE
            My leg!...oh!...I'm ok...no, really I'm...
            Honey!?

ANGLE HORACE, moving forward on cue.

ANGLE JANE AND SHOPKEEPER:

                        SHOPKEEPER
            You ok. No problem.

Holding her stomach gently:

                        JANE
            Yeah...I'm fine...I just hope my baby
            is ok.

The SHOPKEEPER'S jaw drops, as HORACE arrives.

                        HORACE
            Honey, are you allright!? What did they
            do to you!?

                        JANE
            I'm fine. I think.

                        SHOPKEEPER
            She have little fall. No big deal.

>   HORACE
>   Are you sure? Maybe we should report this--
>
>   SHOPKEEPER
>   No report. No problem. Take this for
>   baby. Goodbye. Goodbye.

The SHOPKEEPER gives them a pink mechanical toy duck and the
bum's rush to the door, not noticing HORACE'S exit with the
expensive tie. MUSIC and MONTAGE UP...

27 EXT. CHINATOWN STREETS- NIGHT- LATER

CLOSE UP ON THE DUCK, spinning, flapping wings, whirling
of its own.

REACTIONS CHINATOWN FACES, watching and wondering as...

ANGLE JANE, wide eyed and loving it, miming the motions
of the duck, flapping, spinning, flapping. HORACE just
watching her, all smiles.

28 INT. H & J'S ROOM- NIGHT- LATER

HORACE and JANE in bed, HORACE wears the silkworm tie and
little else, both near naked as they eat Lo Mein noodles,
laughing about the theft, JANE playfully flicks a noodle,
hitting HORACE in the face, who flicks one back at JANE,
more noodles airborne, a full scale food fight begins.

29 INT. H & J'S ROOM- NIGHT- MOMENTS LATER

HORACE and JANE making love in Lo Mein noodles.

30 INT. BATHROOM- NIGHT- STILL LATER

JANE in the tub cleaning up, talking into a tape recorder.

>   JANE
>   Well, I'm just lying here in the tub now.
>   Horace and I have had a wonderful night
>   together. We're planning on doing some-
>   thing tomorrow. I don't know what...
>   (WATER SPLASHING HER)
>   I don't know what else...Stop!

ANGLE HORACE, in the tub with her, doing the splashing.

JANE
(laughing)
I don't know what else to say!--Stop!
STOP!

31 INT. H & J'S ROOM- DAY- A WEEK LATER

WILD MUSIC UP. JANE is alone and set loose upon HORACE'S room.
In a series of MONTAGE cuts, she cleans, dancing with her toy
duck, unpacking her garbage bag full of possessions, hanging
a mirror with fishing line, reading one of HORACE'S under-
ground mags, dancing with the duck some more. OVER:

HORACE(V.O.)
The style now and all at once. Expression
through anarchy.

32 EXT. STREET- DAY- A MONTH LATER

JANE in an outrageous summer outfit running hard at us(as in
the beginning of the FILM) OVER:

HORACE(V.O.)
Helter skelter in crooked heels. Even
watching her catch a bus was new.

33 EXT. PARK- DAY- A WEEK LATER

JANE costumed as an exquisite corpse chained against a tree as
HORACE snaps photos. OVER:

HORACE(V.O.)
Original.

34 EXT. PARK- SAME DAY- LATER

JANE in full makeup, getting a hot dog from a vendor, loading
it up with the works, taking a big bite.

A BOY wanders over to the stand. JANE with a wry smile to him,
pulling out a quarter, doing a sleight-of-hand trick, making
it disappear and reappear behind the BOY'S ear. The BOY
laughing and JANE likewise.

CLOSE ON HORACE, watching JANE. OVER:

HORACE(V.O.)
She was getting to me.

BACK TO JANE, the BOY'S MOTHER calling him and he leaves. The smile on JANE'S face is gone, replaced by a flash of despair, a well of sadness in her revealed.

35   INT. H & J'S ROOM— NIGHT

By candlelight, we see in EXTREME CLOSE UPS, photographs of children. Happy children. Sad children. Haunting children.

CAMERA finds JANE holding up the candle, looking at the photos expressionless, putting the candle down, turning to the bed where HORACE lays in shadow.

> JANE
> Y'see those two in the park today? The
> mother and father? That wind kicking up
> and them just holding each other, kissing,
> whispering like something important was up.
> I was thinking, Hon'. It all blows away,
> doesn't it? Sooner or later. It's kinda,
> kinda an illusion. All of it.
>   (pause)
> I guess there ain't any harm in being
> happy while you can though, huh. Hon'?

HORACE up from shadow, pulling headphones out of his ears, not hearing a word.

> HORACE
> You say something?

JANE with a pause, a sad smile, shaking no.

> HORACE
> Almost done?

Putting on a happy face:

> JANE
> Aha.

Taking the candle up in hand to show her dressed in a sexy French Maid's outfit. HORACE is wide-eyed and ready.

> JANE
> Lights!
>   (CANDLE DOWN)
> Music!
>   (BOOM BOX/MUSIC UP)
> And!

Jane doing a pirouette dance over HORACE, looking magical
as she spins, turns and leaps on him. MUSIC UP and OUT.

36 EXT. HOTEL RIVERVIEW- DAY- ANOTHER WEEK LATER

HORACE waits with a cab at the foot of the hotel stairs, the
meter running, HORACE impatient. OVER:

                    HORACE(V.O.)
          Of course I hadn't met Jane's father. I
          had no way of knowing what his birthday
          meant to her.

Calling up to the front door:

                    HORACE
          Hurry up!

JANE'S head pops out from inside, fumbling bags:

                    JANE
          I am!

                    HORACE
          The meter's running!

                    JANE
          Stop rushin' me!

HORACE up the stairs to help her, JANE p.o.ed as they hurry
down into the cab, it pulls away.

37 INT. CAB- SAME

JANE high strung, wrapping a gift. HORACE confused.

                    HORACE
          You got everything.

                    JANE
          My Dad is particular. You don't get it.
          You just don't get it.

                    HORACE
          I get it--

                    JANE
          This is important to me!

                    HORACE
          Why are you so nervous?

                    JANE
          I'm not nervous!...
                    (pause &)
          I told you. My Dad and I haven't exactly
          seen eye to eye. I wanna show him I'm
          doin' good. I want everything perfect.

                    HORACE
          It will be. Just take it easy. I
          thought he was down in Atlantic City.

                    JANE
          See, you don't listen. We summered
          down the shore. Not lived. Summered.
          Like cultured people do. Take a left.

                    HORACE
          What?

                    JANE
                    (strictly uncultured/to CABBIE)
          LEFT!

The cab swerves left sharply, barely missing other cars and
a red light.

38   EXT. HOTEL BALTIMORE- ALPHABET CITY- MOMENTS LATER

The cab pulls up in front of a trashed awning: HOTEL BALTIMORE.
Two DRUG DEALERS stand beneath.

                    JANE
          This won't take long.

                    HORACE
          What are you doing?

                    JANE
          I gotta pick something up. Charley's
          got valium.

JANE out the door. Stopping her...

                    HORACE
          Wait a minute...

                    JANE
          Baby, I told you about my migraines!
          Like birds in my head. Singin' 'n
          dancin' with those crazy web feet--

JANE is gone before HORACE can react.

39   EXT. HOTEL BALTIMORE- SAME

JANE exchanging greetings with one of the men, CHARLEY, a
greasy industrial waste product, moving off with him through
an alley.

40   INT. CAB- SAME

Looking out with HORACE as JANE disappears down the alley,
is the CABBIE.

                    CABBIE
          She allright? Your girl. She ok?
          I mean she's allright, right? Goin'
          down there with him.
                    (HORACE JUST SHAKES
                    YES THROUGH GLASS)
          Seemed ok. Nice girl. Better than this
          neighborhood.
                    (WATCHING A GANG MEMBER
                    PASS)
          Y'hear they shot a six year old girl
          Thursday? Half a block from here. Stray
          bullet. What do you tell the mother of
          a dead six year old? 'Stray bullet, ma'am.
          Our condolences.' Fuck that. Used to be,
          in this neighborhood, you sneeze at 2 a.m.,
          every window opens 'n you hear: 'God bless
          you.' Now, you're some fucking piece of
          shit, some gangbang scumbag don't-give-a-
          shit-about-my-life-don't-give-a-shit-about-
          yours fuck, not even a beat car around
          to stop you 'n say 'Excuse me, I notice you
          seemed to have missed your fucking bus.' I
          took crash courses in eurology and proctology.
          Just enough to spot an asshole...

CROSSCUTTING between HORACE and the CABBIE, and...

41   EXT. ALLEY- SAME

JANE taking two large purple pills from CHARLEY, swallowing
them.

41A- CHARLEY taking JANE'S money, arguing with her, slapping
JANE twice, JANE hitting back, CHARLEY punching her.

41B- JANE sunken in the alley. CHARLEY walking away.

42   INT. CAB- SAME

HORACE watching the CABBIE open his glove box, revealing a
.38 Special. Pearl handle. Gleaming...

                    CABBIE(O.S.)
        I hope they do. I go to bed hoping.
        They try me. They come at me...

HORACE looking away, in time to see JANE walk to the car,
and right on by...

                    CABBIE(O.S.)
        I got somethin' for them. A fucking--

HORACE out of the cab, chasing JANE down.

                    HORACE
        Jane...hey!...
                (JANE NOT STOPPING,
                GRABBING HER)
        Hey!

                    JANE
        What!?

                    HORACE
        What's wrong?

                    JANE
        Nothin'. Let's get outta here.

                    HORACE
        I asked you a question.

                    JANE
        What do you want me to say!?

                    HORACE
        What's wrong?

                    JANE
                (tears)
        He hit me.

HORACE doesn't understand-- He did what?

                    JANE
        He said I ripped him off! I never did!
        Some bullshit three months ago! I owed
        him!? I never fucking owed him!

Looking for CHARLEY now. Moving:

                    HORACE
        You stay here.

                    JANE
        Where you goin'!? Don't do nothin'.

                    HORACE
I'll be back.

                    JANE
Let's just go.

                    HORACE
I'll be back--

                    JANE
He's got a gun! Allright!?

HORACE stops, pacing, helplessly:

                    HORACE
Oh, great. So I've got a choice. I
can go face a gun or stay here and be a
fucking asshole! What the fuck are
we doing here!?

                    JANE
I won't come back. Honey, I promise.
There's placadil all over town--

                    HORACE
Valium!

                    JANE
What?

                    HORACE
You said valium. For your migraine.
Valium.

                    JANE
So?

He doesn't know, and asks:

                    HORACE
What's placadil?

                    JANE
It's stronger, that's all.

                    HORACE
Let's go to your Dad's.

They move back for the cab.

                    JANE
Can we get a couple drinks before we go?

                    HORACE
          We're an hour late already. You're gonna
          fuck this day up. Or are you <u>trying</u> to
          fuck up?

Stops/p.o.ed:

                    JANE
          I'm not tryin' anything. Why you
          startin' something for?

                    HORACE
          Who's starting, Jane?

                    JANE
          A couple pills? Y'know you worry
          too much. Let me worry about me, ok?
          Talkin' 'bout things you don't under-
          stand.

                    HORACE
          What?

Walking right by him:

                    JANE
          Forget it.

43 EXT. FRONT DOOR- VINCE'S HOME- SAME DAY- LATER

JANE rings the bell, all nerves.

                    JANE
          DADDY!

From within the house an EXPLOSION, six large dogs BARKING
as one. JANE'S father, VINCE, yelling at them from within:

                    VINCE(O.S.)
          SHUT UP! QUIET!

VINCE opens the door fast. Harsh outline of a man. Italian.
Horned rimmed glasses. A well built 72.

                    VINCE
                 (hard/to JANE)
          You're late!

JANE looks to him, tears in eyes.

                    JANE
          Hey you.

As she embraces him, VINCE'S all man exterior seems to
melt away.

HORACE watches it all, wondering-- What the <u>hell</u> is going
on? VINCE and JANE enter, inadvertantly closing the door,
leaving HORACE outside.

44 INT. KITCHEN- DAY- LATER

HORACE sits, JANE hugging the six dogs that rest all around
VINCE.

> VINCE
> Four o'clock--

> JANE
> Chauncey! Chatzee!
> > (to HORACE)
> Chatzee's the one I used to ride like a
> poney!

> VINCE
> That's what you said.

> JANE
> Traffic was murder.

> VINCE
> Four o'clock!

> JANE
> Don't you know anything about rush hour
> traffic!?

> VINCE
> Don't give me a song and dance, Jane Marie!

HORACE attempts to look in the refrigerator. The fattest,
ugliest dog GROWLS.

> JANE
> If you'd seen what we went through
> you'd understand!
> > (to HORACE)
> Tell him, honey. It's a miracle we
> made it at all!

HORACE with no shot at opening his mouth, VINCE back at JANE
immediately.

                    VINCE
          You never been on time a day in your life!

                    JANE
          C'mon Daddy--

                    VINCE
          Just like your mother!

                    JANE
          Daddy!

                    VINCE
          I don't wanna hear it! The lasagna's
          cold in the pan!

To the stove, putting on a tall chef's hat:

                    JANE
          Fear not! Lasagna for three, coming up!

45 INT. KITCHEN- LATER/DAY

JANE, HORACE, VINCE at the table, eating lasagna.

                    JANE
          Daddy's California bound, honey. I
          told you about his ranch house. A
          beautiful split level.

                    HORACE
          How long 'til you finish it?

                    VINCE
          Six months.

                    JANE
          We can go out for visits whenever we
          want. Like raisins roasting in that
          California sun!

                    VINCE
                    (testy)
          Wait'll it's built before you start
          talking about visits.

                    HORACE
          You having trouble with the contractor?

                    VINCE
          My son.

                          JANE
            Daddy hired my brother to do the work.
                     (to VINCE)
            You worry too much.

                          VINCE
            I worry too much?

                          JANE
            He's a professional!

Turning to HORACE for sanity:

                          VINCE
            Until this September my son and I
            hadn't spoken a word to each other in
            ten years. We hadn't agreed on a damn
            thing in twenty five. So what do I
            do? I let him build my house for me.
            That's the story of my life, Harry.

                          HORACE
                     (quietly)
            Horace.

JANE looks to VINCE, to HORACE, with a Cheshire cat smile:

                          JANE
            Let's open gifts.

46   INT. LIVING ROOM- MOMENTS LATER

The television plays b.g., JANE and HORACE wait as VINCE
tries to open JANE'S heavily taped birthday gift, six dogs
at his side.

                          VINCE
            I can't even digest in peace--

                          JANE
            C'mon, open it!

Struggling with the wrapping:

                          VINCE
            I'm trying! You got it wrapped in
            eighty sheets of paper here--

                          JANE
                     (to HORACE)
            Wait'll he sees it! C'mon!

> VINCE
> You're driving me to my grave, Jane
> Marie!

VINCE removes the last of the eighty sheets, JANE watching
in anticipation as he pulls out a large, tacky brass crab.

> JANE
> Isn't he great!

JANE hugs VINCE. The dogs EXPLODE, BARKING wildly.

> VINCE
> (to dogs)
> SHUT UP!

> JANE
> You can add him to your brass collection!

> VINCE
> QUIET!   SHUT UP!

> JANE
> See the way the claws move! And best
> of all...

Taking the crab from VINCE, opening its shell:

> JANE
> He's an ashtray! Just in case company
> drops by, from time to time.

Of course she means herself, yet all VINCE and HORACE can do
is look to each other, speechlessly.

> JANE
> I love him.

47   INT. LIVING ROOM- NIGHT

JANE is asleep, out of nowhere as before, in a contorted pose
on HORACE'S shoulder. VINCE clears away dishes and turns the
TV off before sitting, looking at JANE, at HORACE.

> VINCE
> Do you know what you're getting yourself
> into?

HORACE'S confused look tells VINCE, maybe not.

                    VINCE
        Jane Marie never brought a man to this
        house. You're the first. You two
        serious?

HORACE pauses, as if only now realizing:

                    HORACE
        Yeah, we are.
                    (VINCE EYEING HIM)
        We are.

                    VINCE
        What did she tell you about me?

                    HORACE
        I don't know. She said things haven't
        been good. You had a fight--

                    VINCE
                    (bitter laughter)
        A fight? Yeah, we had a fight! A
        few fights. You'll have a few too.
        And her disappearing act. Be ready
        for that...
                    (recalling)
        I threw her out the last time. For good.
        A couple months ago. Maybe just before
        she picked up with you.

Exactly when they met, though HORACE is silent. The anger
in VINCE has taken him off guard.

                    VINCE
        I was never much of a father. I don't
        put it on anyone else. Jane's mother
        passed away when she was four. After
        that, I don't know, whatever mothers
        and daughters have together, we never
        had that.

                    HORACE
        She doesn't talk about her.

With a pained smile:

                    VINCE
        She don't remember.
                    (pause&...)
        I'll tell you a story and we'll call
        it a night...

CONTINUED:

>   VINCE(CONT.)
>   When Jane Marie turned twenty-one she
>   disappeared off the face of the earth.
>   It took her four weeks to go through a
>   trust fund I'd set up for her. 20,000
>   dollars in four weeks. And when it
>   was gone she came to me crying. Her
>   arms were black and blue. Needle
>   marks. Like a pin cushion. She
>   said she couldn't stop. Couldn't.
>   Wouldn't. Who cares. So you know
>   what I'd do? Every night I'd drive
>   her up to a park in the South Bronx.
>   I'd stay in the car and watch her
>   crowd in with them. The walking dead.
>   That's what I called them. Junkies.
>   Thieves. Like scum in the street.
>   I'd stay in the car 'til she did what
>   she had to do. Then we'd leave. I
>   don't know why I went along with it or
>   why I stopped. I just know I couldn't
>   stand to see her in pain. I couldn't
>   stand it.

VINCE'S macho demeanor has crumbled, his words like a
thunderbolt to HORACE, who looks back to VINCE without
blinking.

48   EXT. CAB- LATE NIGHT

In front of the Hotel Lombard, JANE still passed out, HORACE
lifting her out of the cab, up into his arms.

49   INT. H & J'S ROOM- A MOMENT LATER

HORACE lays JANE down. Looking her over. On his face, the
images and weight of VINCE'S words. OVER:

>   HORACE(V.O.)
>   Kick around in the darkness long
>   enough, the darkness will find you.

50   EXT. HOTEL LOMBARD- DAY

HORACE off to work, JANE waving goodbye from their porthole
window. HORACE hardly seems to notice, walking out over
a building SOUND of New York.

LONG SHOT. JANE waving from the window. HORACE walking
to work. Two dots in a gray landscape.

51 INT. H & J'S ROOM- DAY

A MONTAGE OF CUTS...

JANE making the bed, cleaning the room, listening to
and repeating phrases from a LEARN TO SPEAK FRENCH
record from Rudy's room.

51A- JANE laid out on the bed. Watching TV with little
interest. The French record still filters in. JANE
no longer following the phrases.

51B- JANE pacing the room, bored, waiting for HORACE.
Looking into a mirror. Not liking what looks back. The
French record still plays. (*The humor of the tiny room
has giving way to a feel of solitary confinement, utter
claustrophobia*)

52 INT. H & J'S ROOM- NIGHT

The TV plays but JANE isn't watching. Her expression utterly
vacant. Staring at the wall collage...

CLOSE UPS, PHOTOS: More children. Sad. Happy. Haunting.
In sight and SOUND, seeming to come alive, CHILDREN'S VOICES
and LAUGHTER...

CLOSE ON JANE, turning away, toward a stuffed animal on the
dresser-- A thought gnawing at her, a war for control underway.
SOUND of TV deafening. SOUND of the FRENCH record a nightmare.

53 INT. THE DUMPLING HOUSE- SAME NIGHT- LATER

FLASH of JANE among wreckage. Torched dragon decor.
Hundreds of Chinese menus on the floor. Bending on her
knees. To her belly. Finding a crawlhole and crawling,
disappearing through it.

54 INT. H & J'S ROOM- SAME NIGHT- VERY LATE

HORACE arrives home to find TV LIGHT and... JANE... on the
floor, unconscious. A sick feeling in HORACE before seeing
her breathe, her face in a bowl of soup, HORACE taking a
breath himself, moving to her.

[PAGE 42 OMITTED]

HORACE moving down hotel stairs to work, as we...

MATCH DISSOLVE TO:
58 EXT. HOTEL LOMBARD- SAME NIGHT

HORACE returning home from work, up the stairs.

59 INT. H & J'S ROOM- SAME

HORACE opening the door, not sure what he'll find this time,
seeing... The room is empty. JANE is gone. Recalling VINCE'S
words. OVER:

                    HORACE(V.O.)
          I used to talk to God.

60 INT. AMPITHEATER- DAY

HORACE in the burned out hellhole and fake Roman ruins, same
ruins JANE showed him, still fantastically otherwordly yet
ugly now, and dangerous, used/bloody needles litter the floor,
JUNKIES shuttling in and out and HORACE alone, his look and
manner are death, searching for JANE. OVER:

                    HORACE(V.O.)
          You know how you get down on your knees
          or you look to the sky. And you talk
          to God. When you're down.

61 EXT. HOTEL SUNSHINE- AFTERNOON

CHARLEY and his PAL stand out front as HORACE approaches,
questions about JANE lead to fingerpointing and pushing,
CHARLEY'S PAL breaking them apart, motioning toward cops,
CHARLEY and PAL back off with curses, HORACE with no answers.
OVER:

                    HORACE(V.O.)
          It's something you do. You know you're
          not going to get through but you do it
          anyway. It makes you feel better.

62 INT. H & J'S ROOM- NIGHT

RAPID SHOTS...

HORACE still and sleepless on the bed, staring upwards.
Hellish NOISE from other rooms crowds in on him. The room
an absolute prison cell.

62A- HORACE watches TV. Looking right through it. Absently changing channels, faster, <u>faster</u>. Images collide, coalescing in his mind.

62B- HORACE on the bed, watching... a cockroach emerge. From a corner. HORACE moves to it. Picking up a heavy book and watching... <u>Dozens of cockroaches</u> scattering. HORACE startled a moment, then furiously, crushing them with the book, with his bare hands, splattering them against photos on the wall.

62C- HORACE looking at JANE'S stuffed animal, the sewing come undone, <u>something falling out</u>. He picks it up. OVER:

> HORACE(V.O)
> You talk to God like you would to a
> bartender, like a confessor. God of
> waterfalls and forests. Fire and ice.
> The perfect God. He was everywhere.
> Everything was as it was for a purpose.

63 INT. DUMPLING HOUSE- NEXT DAY

CAMERA TRACKING up through the burnt out Chinese restuarant, 1st floor, OVER:

> HORACE(V.O.)
> I used to ask him for someone I could be
> close to. Someone who would be there when
> the world came to take me out.

TRACKING up through the crawlspace, through 2nd floor rubble and twisting corners, out a window and up a fire escape to the 3rd floor. This can only be described as a war zone. Nothing resembling furniture. Only a transistor RADIO, playing aimlessly...

CAMERA CLOSING ON A FIGURE, laid out in a corner....

CAMERA CLOSING ON JANE, HER EYES rolled back, the hit arrived OVER:

> HORACE(V.O.)
> And the time came when I thought he
> delivered. It seemed that way.

64 INT. DUMPLING HOUSE- SAME DAY- LATER

JANE'S friend, LUCINDA, near a window when a rock hits it...

LUCINDA looks to the window and away. A second rock breaks
the window. LUCINDA opens up, looking down...

ANGLE 3RD FLOOR, HORACE below, calling up....

                    HORACE
          Is she there!? DID YOU SEE HER!?

LUCINDA shakes no, closing the window abruptly, turning...

P.O.V, JANE passed out. A shabby wool cover over her.

ANGLE BELOW, HORACE trying to climb the fire escape, unable
to pull it down, pounding at the door of the Dumpling House,
moving off disgusted. OVER:

                    HORACE(V.O.)
          But he missed the mark again.

65 EXT. PARK- SAME DAY- LATE AFTERNOON

Pigeons scatter against the sky. HORACE sits on a bench,
staring off as a MAN feeds the birds, and we:

MATCH DISSOLVES:
65A EXT. PARK- SAME

Day giving way to night. Night to day. HORACE hasn't moved
from the bench.

66 INT. H & J'S ROOM- 3RD NIGHT- 5 A.M.

DARKNESS. Discordant SOUND from a harmonica.

SOUND from outside the door. A key put into an unlocked
door, locking it. JANE curses. Struggling to get inside.
OVER:

                    HORACE(V.O.)
          In the end my God of perfection missed
          by an inch.

LIGHTS switch on. JANE sees HORACE in bed, wide awake,
putting down the harmonica. JANE stumbles in...this a second
JANE, the "East Side" JANE, a stranger to HORACE, utterly
trashed and seeking no forgiveness, struggling only to take
her jacket off.

                    HORACE
          Where were you?

                    JANE
          I went for drinks. What's with you?

                    HORACE
          It's been three days.

                    JANE
          So. Whaddya want me to do, watch TV
          every night?

                    HORACE
          I didn't say that.

                    JANE
          Good....'cause I'm not doin' it.

Up from bed, barely containing himself:

                    HORACE
          Who were you with?

                    JANE
          Nobody...you'd know.

                    HORACE
          You stop by Charley's, for your pill fix?

                    JANE
                  (smiling)
          You are what you eat, baby.

                    HORACE
          I'll tell you what, Jane. I found
          something interesting last night.

HORACE reaches for her stuffed animal, into the stuffing,
pulling out a box, opening it to show: <u>Needle and works</u>.

                    HORACE
          Stuffing fell out.

                    JANE
                  (ice)
          Fell out, huh. It's not mine.

                    HORACE
          No, you're holding it for someone--

                    JANE
          Look, it's not mine, man! And I don't
          like you goin' through my stuff! You
          get your kicks doin' that!? I don't
          want you doin' that again!

                     HORACE
          You been shootin' the whole time?

                      JANE
          I haven't in months! Because of you!
          You're so fucking blind!

                     HORACE
          You're full of shit.

                       JANE
          Please!

                     HORACE
          You been busted, baby.

                       JANE
          You didn't bust me--

                       HORACE
          I BUSTED YOU!

                       JANE
          YOU DIDN'T BUST ME! NOBODY BUSTS ME!

HORACE swipes the dresser top, JANE'S perfumes, stuffed animals,
jewelry, knocking her over. JANE comes back at HORACE, smashing
him full face...

CLOSE ON HORACE, stunned, furious and then, a smile, waiting
for another...

CLOSE ON JANE, hitting him harder... This one shaking <u>her</u>
out of it. Kissing HORACE quickly. He pulls her away,
with a smile...

                     HORACE
          Your father was right. Like scum
          in the street.

                       JANE
          FUCK YOU! FUCK BOTH'YA'S! I'M NOT
          SORRY!

HORACE moving for a bag, packing. JANE to bed, watching him.

                       JANE
          Yeh, y'know, you should see yerself.
          Way your face tightens up like that.
          You get ugly. I can't even look at you
          like that.

SILENCE. HORACE packing.

> JANE
> Where'ya goin'? Taking a little trip?
> (NO ANSWER)
> Whatcha doin', do tell?
> (NO ANSWER)
> Now you don't talk.
> (NO ANSWER)
> Listen, Hon'...hey...don't go crazy on me.

Closing the half packed case, moving, for the door:

> HORACE
> I'll get the rest tomorrow.

> JANE
> Baby...

A softening in her voice, the JANE he knows seeming to emerge, beginning to cry. HORACE stops at the door.

> HORACE
> I can't.
> (pause/realizing)
> You know I love you? I love you, Jane.

> JANE
> Don't go.

HORACE back in from the door. To Jane. Holding each other. Lost, truly lost:

> HORACE
> I don't know what to do. Tell me what
> to do.

The SCREEN FLASHING to WHITE, with VOICES...

> JANE(V.O.)
> There should be something deep between us.

> HORACE(V.O.)
> I suggest...the Atlantic Ocean.

FADE UP ON:
67 EXT. THE BOARDWALK- ATLANTIC CITY- BRIGHT DAY- A SINGLE GULL

Squawking, jumping its perch, flying up and over as JANE and HORACE...

...turn off the Boardwalk, toward...

68   EXT. PRINCETON ANTIQUES/ROOMINGHOUSE- DAY- A MOMENT LATER

A MOTEL MAN opens up on a small 1 BR apartment. Plug ugly.
Dirty windows. Stripped kitchen and bathroom. Zero
personality. HORACE looks to JANE who looks away, looking
flat out sick.

> MOTEL MAN
> Week or month?

Pause, and:

> HORACE
> Month.

69   INT. H & J'S ROOM- THE PRINCETON- NIGHT

HORACE outside the bathroom. SOUND of puking within. JANE
opens the door and exits without looking at the concerned
HORACE.

70   INT. H & J'S ROOM- DAYS LATER

HORACE enters with ice bucket and brown bag, bending over
JANE who is layed out in bed, feverish, looking awful.
HORACE pressing a cold compress to her head.

> JANE
> Didja get it?

> HORACE
> I got it.

Breaking out from the bag, a jar of baby food: Gerber's Pears.
Feeding it to her:

> HORACE
> You should be eating real food.

> JANE
> You'd be wearing it.

> HORACE
> It's the years of shit catching up with
> you. Beginning to play some rough tricks.

                  JANE
No sermons, please. I get enough
at the clinic.

                  HORACE
How's the methadone? Strong?

                  JANE
Beats tequila. Try a thimble full. You'll
be out two days.
                  (&)
I knew a girl on methadone. She got high
on aspirin. Took about 80 a day. She'd
be watching TV 'n a commercial for Bayer
or Anacin would come on. She'd get
weird.

                  HORACE
Let's see what we got.

Sticking a thermometer in her mouth. Up to look out a window:

                  HORACE
The beach is nice. All the times I
been down here, I never saw it. I was
always in the casino.

                  JANE
I'm gonna go--

                  HORACE
You're gonna forget about it, I told you--

                  JANE
C'mon!

                  HORACE
You're sick! You need to see!?

Taking a large mirror off the wall, turning it on JANE, who
ducks the sick reflection.

                  HORACE
Yes, ladies and gents, there she is,
Miss New Jersey! Beauty, grace, a pretty
face. Don't be intimdated by her, folks,
sixty milligrams of methadone would curl
your hair too. She brushes her teeth
three times a day, I have that on good
authority. Our very own Baby Jane.
Wants to play in the sand with...

Checking the thermometer, with seriousness.

>   HORACE
>   Yes, temperature 103. Up another
>   degree.

JANE sinks back down on the bed. HORACE brushes away sweat,
with love.

>   HORACE
>   Some kid.

71   INT. H & J'S ROOM- SAME NIGHT- 4 A.M.

CAMERA PANS JANE in a feverish sweat, tossing in bad sleep, a
near delirium, CAMERA finding HORACE beside her, wide awake
and with real concern, thinking hospital.

72   EXT. BEACH- DAYS LATER- EARLY EVENING

CLOSE ON JANE, fever broken but weak, with an expression of joy,
looking up to the sun.

CLOSE ON HORACE, watching her.

>   JANE
>   Nice.

WIDER TO SHOW, HORACE and JANE on the beach. The whole of
ATLANTIC CITY before them. Casino/hotels. The Boardwalk,
sand and ocean. A stark beauty. JANE shaky, taking
HORACE'S hand, moving down an empty stretch of beach in
a five color sunset.

73   EXT. BOARDWALK BENCH AREA- MOMENTS LATER

HORACE on a bench, relaxing. Behind him are VOICES:

>   MAN 1(O.S.)
>   ...Shirley Temple? I had a Shirley Temple
>   thing when I was a kid. Best ass I ever
>   saw.

>   WOMAN 1(O.S.)
>   That's pathetic, Joe.

>   MAN 1(O.S.)
>   When she was a teenager! Her teenage
>   movies. Fort Apache. That Hagan Girl.
>   The broad had a great ass. That's all
>   I'm sayin'.

                    MAN 2(O.S.)
          You mean her kiddy flicks don't arouse
          you?

                    MAN 1(O.S.)
          Arouse me? You're sick, y'know that.

HORACE turns to see...on benches, two couples: WOMAN 1 eats
pink cotton candy. MAN 1 fudge. WOMAN 2 a foot long hot dog.
MAN 2 pizza. HORACE watches them lick and chew.

                    WOMAN 2
          Don't point fingers, Frank. Y'know what
          handsome did as a kid?

                    WOMAN 1
          What?

                    WOMAN 2
          He'd come down the shore weekends. Feed
          Bromo Seltzer to the seagulls. Their
          stomachs would explode. They'd come
          crashing to the ground.

The MEN laughing, the WOMEN back to licking and chewing as
HORACE looks away, over to...

ANGLE JANE, licking an ice cream cone in an identical manner,
same rhythm as the locals. Innocently, to HORACE:

                    JANE
          So, what now?

A FLOCK OF SEAGULLS takes to the sky, as if afraid of what's
about to follow. WILD MUSIC UP, and a MONTAGE:

74 EXT. MARGATE BEACH- SUNNY DAY

HORACE and JANE at the beach. Incredibly, we see JANE'S
full body without a head. HORACE is just a head, utterly
bodiless! JANE spoils the illusion by rising for a drink
drink of water, sipping some and passing it to HORACE who
(we can now see) is buried in sand. JANE runs off leaving
HORACE in up to the neck, unconcerned, grabbing some sun.

75 EXT. LUCY THE ELEPHANT- MARGATE BEACH- SAME DAY

JANE looking up at Lucy(a 90-foot red and grey concrete
elephant once used as a hotel). HORACE snaps a photo.

76 EXT. BOARDWALK- MARGATE BEACH- SAME DAY

JANE gets the lowdown on a stick of regenerating wood from a
Boardwalk booth SALESMAN. HORACE skeptical among several
blossomed sticks.

77 EXT. MARGATE BEACH- SAME DAY- SUNSET

LONG SHOT. JANE and HORACE walk Margate Beach, a magic
sunset before them.

78 EXT. UNDER GARDEN PIER- DAY- A WEEK LATER

JANE posing for another "death" photo in a labyrinth of wooden
pylons. Decked out in white wedding dress, tied by thick rope
to a pylon with a knife plugged into her neck. HORACE with
camera, snapping away.

CLOSE ON JANE, doing her best but breaking up laughing.

HORACE laughing, moving to her. They kiss. Steel Pier and
Atlantic Ocean at play behind them.

79 EXT. BOARDWALK- SAME DAY- LATER

CLOSE ON HORACE AND JANE seated, JANE still in white wedding
dress, Boardwalk scenery passes, a sense of motion. HORACE beat,
JANE excited, reaching into a bag.

                         JANE
                Check it out! A shark fetus! What a
                great gift!

                         HORACE
                       (disgusted)
                Shark fetus?

                         JANE
                For my Dad! And look what else...
                       (REACHING IN)
                Pecan turtles! Mmmm! Check it out,
                they really look like turtles. It was
                either them or the macadamia clusters
                the macadamia clusters. You believe
                they wanted seven dollars a pound for
                'em? That's a lot of macadamias.

                         HORACE
                       (not listening)
                You got that right.

                    JANE
Honey, I was on Atlantic Avenue before.
I saw some two tone pants in the Mall.
Designer label. Two pairs, seventeen
dollars! We can't pass up bargains
like that!

                    HORACE
We don't have the cash.

                    JANE
Don't worry. I'm calling my Dad today.

                    HORACE
You're taking more money off him?

                    JANE
I gotta!

                    HORACE
He just sent down 200.

                    JANE
Just 'til I get on my feet! I've been
looking for work, right?

                    HORACE
Is that what you call it?

                    JANE
I have been looking!

                    HORACE
Sure, sure.

                    JANE
                (truly p.o.ed)
For your information Mr. Tranvestite Bar,
Mr. Vibrating Pillow Salesman-- I looked
in the want ads 2 hours yesterday.

                    HORACE
Woow. Hit a nerve, baby?

                    JANE
You and my father! Neither of yas think
I can do it, right!?

                    HORACE
I never said you couldn't do it. I just
said I don't know many employers hiring
people who who show up to the interview
in their bathing suit--

Really p.o.ed now:

> JANE
> I never did that!

> HORACE
> It's a joke! I was kidding!

> JANE
> G'head, kid! Have fun. We'll see
> who's laughing soon enough.

Changing subject:

> HORACE
> So how's he doing, your Dad?

Thinking about VINCE, a smile, nostalgic at once.

> JANE
> He's gettin' ready to move. The ranch-
> house is coming along. He sent some
> pictures. It's beautiful. Maybe another
> month or two to finish it.

> HORACE
> And?

> JANE
> (sadly)
> He said he's happy. He's happy 'cause
> I'm happy. I told him I was lookin'
> good, y'know, feeling good. And he
> said he proud of me. That's what he
> said. He was proud of me.
> (choking up)
> I'm gonna miss him.

> HORACE
> I know.

> JANE
> Every time I go away I think I'm never
> gonna see him again. He's a 72 year old
> man.

> HORACE
> Hey...

JANE is crying.

                    HORACE
Hey ...c'mon!
          (HOLDS HER)
We're having a good time and you start
crying!?

                    JANE
I can't help it.

                    HORACE
I know. You get emotional.
          (caresses her face)
We had to get out of there.
          (squeezes her cheeks
          playfully)
Where would we be if we were still at
the Lombard? Where would you be?

                    JANE
          (childlike)
Dead.

                    HORACE
Maybe.

                    JANE
You saved me.

                    HORACE
I took you on a bus ride.

                    JANE
You did more than that.
          (kissing him)
More than you know.

                    HORACE
Pop me a macadamia cluster!

                    JANE
A pecan turtle! I told you.

WIDER TO SHOW, they are riding in a Boardwalk rolling chair.
JANE spying a fancy Boardwalk store.

                    JANE
Where do we get off?

                    HORACE
End of the line.

                    JANE
          Honey, remember the fortune teller I
          talked with last week?

                    HORACE
          Yeah.

                    JANE
          I wasn't supposed to divulge this, y'
          understand. You know about messin' with
          the Mysteries and Fate and whatnot--

                    HORACE
                (sensing a Jane angle)
          Aha.

                    JANE
                (mysteriously)
          She told me I had to get you inside that
          store today. Inside there they've got
          a giant Mr. Peanut scale. He's got a
          monocle over one eye. Real distinguished.
          And you go right up to him, deposit a
          quarter and read your weight on the top
          of his tophat. But that's not all.
          Then he reaches down with a moveable arm,
          right down into his shell, and hands you
          a peanut. This is no ordinary peanut.
          Inside is a hand-written fortune that's
          never wrong.
                (to ROLLING CHAIR MAN)
          We'll get out here, Mister!
                (to HORACE)
          The fortune teller said you must do this.
          Today. Right now. Your whole future
          depends on it!

     HORACE not believing a word of it, not moving.

                    JANE
          Come inside with me and step up on Mr.
          Peanut! C'mon, honey!

     HORACE laughing as JANE takes his legs, trying to drag him
     off the rolling chair.

                    JANE
          Just one more store! Honeeeeeeeey!

     80   INT. H & J'S ROOM- NIGHT

The filthy, depressing space has taken on new life as JANE
happily overcooks a blob of spaghetti, dancing with the duck,
reaching into its bill and eating jellybeans, overheated,
fanning herself. OVER:

                    HORACE(V.O.)
          Home was something more than what I came
          back to nights. It was the spilling out
          of her life. The Rembrandt in Jane's
          mind.

RAPID CLOSE SHOTS of some of the following...

                    HORACE(V.O.)
          Her combs and empty Tylenol bottles.
          The brass bulldog and unicorn, cockle-
          shells, crystals, earrings, buttons,
          aspirins, nuts. Snapshots of her father
          and I in .49 cent plastic holders. The
          dead cactus she wouldn't throw out.
          Oriental wind chimes and ceramic dogs
          and refrigerator magnets. The butter
          cut longways. The five pound bags of
          sugar. The clothes scattered on chairs,
          in the kitchen sink. The stuff was
          piling up on all sides. Everywhere.
          I got the idea Jane liked it that way.

HORACE enters, not noticing JANE'S chaotic movements, setting
down a deli bag at the table and sitting, dead tired. OVER:

                    HORACE(V.O.)
          She was born for the domestic life.

                    JANE
          Hey you! The toilet's backed up...

HORACE with a beaten down glance at JANE, moving to the bathroom without a word.

                    JANE
          Something's jammed!

ANGLE TOILET BOWL, HORACE looking down inside, seeing...
something... reaching down inside...

                    JANE(O.S.)
          So how was work?

ANGLE JANE, over the stove, draining the spaghetti which comes out in a single clump.

> JANE
> I'm cookin' sketties. You hungry?

> HORACE(O.S.)
> I ate.

ANGLE BATHROOM:

> JANE(O.S.)
> More pastrami? You should wait 'til you
> get home! Nice home cooked meal!

HORACE feeling something...reaching down even deeper... yanking it out...

ANGLE KITCHEN, HORACE emerges with a jar of cold creme.

> JANE
> My hero! Is that where my cold creme
> went!?

HORACE makes a face, putting down the jar, moving off.

> JANE
> You won't believe my day! Anything
> happen with you!?

HORACE layed out in bed, going through bills, stopping and looking at an advertising flyer from a casino school, with a spooked face.

> HORACE
> No.

CUT TO:
81 EXT. JITNEY STOP- SAME DAY- HOURS BEFORE

HORACE sits on a bench waiting for a jitney(bus). A MAN, JOHNNY BIANCHI, nervously paces, stops, looks off, sitting no more than a second, up again, pacing.

> BIANCHI
> Bullshit.

Offering a pack of cigarettes to HORACE, who shakes no. BIANCHI lights up.

> BIANCHI
> Goddamn jitneys, huh.

HORACE a bit uncomfortable, looking away.

                    BIANCHI
          Got a '95 turbo Porsche in the shop.
          I gotta sit here like a mope waiting
          on a jitney.

HORACE with no response, which doesn't stop BIANCHI...

                    BIANCHI
          You know what Einstein said? He said God
          doesn't roll dice. What does that mean
          to you?
                    (HORACE SILENT)
          Exactly. Don't mean shit to me neither.
          Means Einstein knew gatz about dice.
          Einstein was a mope is what it means.
          Know what my philosophy is? My '95
          Porsche, know what the licence plate
          says?

In HORACE'S face, BIANCHI snaps...

CLOSE ON A 100 DOLLAR BILL, the new design, peeling it back
into a thick wallet:

                    BIANCHI
          ...C-NOTE. That's right. That's my
          philosophy. You got money, you rate.
          You don't, you're a putz.
                    (&)
          You'd like my car. Nice car. I love it.
          But I'd trade it in tomorrow. Wouldn't mean
          a thing to me. Why? It's a trap. Like
          a guy's house. His car. His wife. Just
          traps in the end. Take my wife. Great
          broad. People think I'm lucky to have
          her. They can't see my wife and I maybe
          have a few problems. A few major fucking
          problems. They don't know. They don't
          know the only reason I keep her around
          is to wash my shirts. Things are never
          as they seem. Remember that.

HORACE is speechless, and BIANCHI goes on...

                    BIANCHI
          Take a guy waiting on a street corner.
          Light changes. He crosses the street.
          Goes on his way. 2nd guy waits on the
          same corner. Light changes. He crosses
          and WHAM!...
                    (HORACE JUMPS)
          Hit by a city sanitation truck...

CONTINUED:

                    BIANCHI(CONT.)
          Big blue. Pennsylvania steel. First guy
          is clear. Second guy is roadkill. <u>Why</u>?
          I mean, why? Who the fuck knows why.
                    (and)
          Fuck this shit.

BIANCHI handing HORACE a card, walking off.

                    BIANCHI
          Look me up sometime. I'll change your
          life.

CUT BACK TO:
82 INT. H & J'S ROOM- A MOMENT LATER

HORACE holds up the card.

INSERT CARD: JOHNNY BIANCHI--"THE KING OF CRAPS"-- CRAPS
                    INSTRUCTOR: MILTON CASINO SCHOOL

HORACE holds up the flyer.

INSERT FLYER: MILTON CASINO SCHOOL--ENROLL NOW!

HORACE is too tired to contemplate fate vs. coincidence, as...

WHAM!

JANE jumps him! On the bed, cuddling. HORACE startled,
looking back to the flyer and card.

                    JANE
          You gonna do it? Casino work is big bucks.

                    HORACE
          I don't know.

                    JANE
          We could get an air-conditioner. It's
          getting ridiculous with the heat.

                    HORACE
          You spend too much time cooking spaghetti.

                    JANE
          Don't you worry about my 'sketties.
          I can cook y'know.

                    HORACE
          Oh sure. That Oriental noodle soup.
          You do that great. Boil 'n serve.

                    JANE
                  (smiling)
     Stop.

                    HORACE
     And creamed corn as a main course. How
     can you forget meals like that?

                    JANE
     Whaddya expect on the money you bring
     home!?

                    HORACE
     Hey! I'm a good provider.

                    JANE
     Yeah, and they call me Pocahontas.

Trying to grab, kiss her:

                    HORACE
     Glad ta meetcha, Princess--

They wrestle, hand to hand combat, kissing, JANE breaking
away, eyes widening, reaching to HORACE'S back.

                    HORACE
     Jane. Don't--

                    JANE
     Honey, you got...4...5 blackheads--

                    HORACE
     Jane--

                    JANE
     And look at the whiteheads!

                    HORACE
     STOP!...

In a life and death struggle, leaping from her clutches:

                    HORACE
     I LIKE MY SKIN THE WAY IT IS!

                    JANE
     WHAT A BABY! JEZ!

Collapsing back in bed:

                    HORACE
          Christ, I'm beat.

                    JANE
               (CUDDLING W/HIM)
          Well I got news for you, since you
          didn't ask about my day. I got
          a job!
               (HORACE AMAZED/JANE BEAMING)
          This guy Dan. He runs the cheesesteak
          place on Fairmont. He said come down
          Saturday. We'd get a part-time thing
          going. It'd be 6 an hour! Under the
          table!

                    HORACE
          Allright!

                    JANE
          Told you! Told you I'd do it!
               (&)
          And guess what else!

Rising, to show the stick of regenerated wood planted, a
single green bud emerging.

                    JANE
          Look at Stick! He sprouted last night!
          Right there! He's growing! Our baby!

HORACE just smiling, amazed at JANE, who caresses the stick,
caressing HORACE.

                    JANE
          Who knows. Maybe some day we can grow
          our own baby.

HORACE gets her intention, wanting nothing to do with it, yawns:

                    HORACE
          Jesus, I'm tired. Guess it's just
          about bedtime, huh?

JANE punching him, moving off.

                    HORACE
          Ey!

Angrier than she's showing, JANE back at the spaghetti without
a word.

                    HORACE
         What!? Lay down here with me!

                     JANE
         Lay there yourself! Baby hater!

                    HORACE
         I don't hate babies! Like W.C. Fields
         said: I love kids, medium rare.

A kitchen utensil flies at HORACE, just missing him. Laughing:

                    HORACE
         Ey! Easy, Susie Homemaker!

As HORACE turns his back, JANE lightens up, sneaking up
behind him, leaping in the air with karate chop...

                     JANE
         AYYYYYYYAAAA!

CUT TO:
83 INT. CLASSROOM— CRAPS SCHOOL— DAY

PAN white numbers on the green felt of a craps table.
With a VOICE:

                   BIANCHI(O.S.)
         So. Here we are. This is craps.
         You wanted it. You got it.

ANGLE JOHNNY BIANCHI, the "King of Craps", holding court.
Several STUDENTS surround him and the table, HORACE among
them. With a Vegas smile:

                    BIANCHI
         Let me tell you a little something about
         myself. My name is Johnny Bianchi...
         I was brought up in a Pennsylvania steel-
         town in a family of eleven. My father
         was a factory worker. My brothers are
         factory workers. I was never a factory
         worker. Everything I am I owe to craps.
         I love this business. As a craps
         instructor, I've trained 600 good eggs.
         I told every one of them just what I'm
         abot to tell you.
                   (Vegas smile)
         It's time to get smart, people! The
         possibilities for you in this business
         are unlimited! When somebody asks me
         about my goals, about my dreams, you
         know what I tell 'em? Nothing. I set
         my goals so high I don't tell anyone.
         You know why? They'd laugh at me...

              [PAGE 65 OMITTED]

DAN hits the door, gone. JANE fixes her tophat, checks a
mirror, the reflection shows pure happiness, but nervous,
her first job in years, pulling at a sliver of cheese,
looking out the window, chewing, as we:

CUT BACK TO:
85   INT. CASINO SCHOOL- DAY- LATER

STUDENTS have formed a line across from BIANCHI at the
crapstable.

                    BIANCHI
          I won't repeat the call, people.
                    (methodically)
          Winner 7. Front Line Winner. Take the
          Don'ts. Pay the Front. Working bets
          have action. Save the odds. Pay behind.
                    (snaps fingers)
          Let's go. Once with feeling.

STUDENT 1 steps up, takes the Stickman's stick in hand.

                    STUDENT 1
                    (weakly)
          Winner 7. Front Line Winner. Take the
          Don'ts--

                    BIANCHI
          LOUDER! When you stand in there as a
          Stickman you gotta be heard! The meek
          may inherit the earth but they got no
          business in the craps pit! Next.

STUDENT 2 steps up, picks up the stick, and...

                    STUDENT 2
          Winner! Winner Front Line! Pay the
          Do's! Save the behind!

                    BIANCHI
          WINNER 7 WINNER 7 WINNER 7! Front Line
          Winner! Excitement, people! That's
          what it's about! Next.

STUDENT 3 steps up.

                    STUDENT 3
          WIENER 7! FRONT LINE WIENER!

                    BIANCHI
          NEXT!

HORACE steps up, picking up the Stickman's stick. BIANCHI moving across the table, in his face:

                    BIANCHI
          Allright, coz. Look at me. Look in my
          eyes.

BIANCHI with a laughable intensity, as HORACE looks in his eyes, barely able to keep a straight face.

                    BIANCHI
          Now lemme have it, Bubba! Gimme
          everything ya got!

HORACE'S look is expressionless wonder, as we:

CUT BACK TO:
86 INT. SUB SHOP- SAME

CHAOS. JANE cutting Italian beef rapidly. A pot boils over, overflows on the stove. The telephone <u>RINGING</u>. JANE panicking.

87 EXT. SUB SHOP- SAME

Sedate Boardwalk activity. TOURISTS pass routinely when... from inside the shop, behind the cheesesteak and snowcone colored awning, a HOWLING CRY.

                    JANE(O.S.)
          Owww, fuck!

88 INT. SUB SHOP- SAME

CLOSE ON JANE'S FACE, wailing like a baby:

                    JANE
          FUUUUUUUUUCK!

CUT TO:
89 INT. SUB SHOP- LATER

HORACE flying in through the front door:

                    HORACE
          What the fuck?

DAN has returned, JANE rushing to HORACE in tears, a big Ace bandage wrapped around her thumb.

                    HORACE
What happened?

                    DAN
She lost a tip. No big deal.
It happens all the time. Look...

DAN shows his fingers, several fingertips gone. HORACE looks
back at him in disbelief.

                    JANE
I was just cutting some extra meat and--

                    DAN
She's a good worker. I'd hate to lose her
'cause of a little accident. There's no
summer help in this town. Local kids
won't work for minimum wage. I'm chained
in here 80 hours a week.
               (to HORACE)
Who can ya trust nowadays? Tell me.
Who can ya trust?

DAN looks to HORACE. HORACE to DAN, to JANE. Nothing more
any of them can do.

90   INT. H & J'S ROOM- NIGHT

HORACE laughing at his typewriter, JANE soaking her thumb in
iodine. OVER:

                    HORACE(V.O.)
She was bandaged from that one for weeks.
I always wondered about the piece of her
thumb that was lost among the dehydrated
onions. They never did recover it.

HORACE waving for JANE to read something, not seeing JANE
is disgusted, wondering-- What's wrong with her? Can't even
hold a shitty job, why?-- depressed and wincing in the iodine.

91   INT. SANDS CASINO GAZEBO- ARKANSAS AVENUE- EARLY EVENING

JANE in a bright gold Camera Girl outfit, standing against old
neon Altantic City signs--The 500 Club, Club Harlem, Steel Pier--
the bright neon signs and her bright outfit contrast with her
face...which is devastated. OVER:

                    HORACE(V.O.)
Not long after she worked as a Camera
Girl before getting fired for smoking
on the job.

92   EXT. GAZEBO- SAME

JANE emerging, onto the Boardwalk, passing happy TOURISTS
as the tears begin to come. Walking square into FRAME,
her face is frightening. OVER:

> HORACE(V.O.)
> After that she stopped looking for
> work.

93   INT. STAIRCASE- THE PRINCETON- NIGHT

HORACE returning from work, up the narrow stairs. OVER:

> HORACE(V.O.)
> Many nights I'd find her on the floor,
> asleep in impossible positions. The
> ends of Pop Tarts on the rug. An
> untouched cup of tea beside her.

94   INT. INTERIOR HALLWAY- THE PRINCETON- NIGHT

HORACE moves down the hall, opening his door. OVER:

> HORACE(V.O.)
> Other times I'd find something very
> different.

JANE is gone. The room empty. HORACE recalling New York,
her "disappearing act", cursing, moving back out the door.
CROSSCUTTING begins between HORACE, and...

95   EXT. MR. O'S- NIGHT- SAME MOMENT

A local "dirt" bar, JANE wanting to drink the pain away,
moving for the door. A SWEATING MAN sees her.

> SWEATING MAN
> Hey.

Holding the door closed. Utterly unintimidated:

> JANE
> Get outta my way.

> SWEATING MAN
> (w/more meaning)
> You need somethin'?

Knowing what he means, JANE pauses, looking up at him a first
time, hard and fast.

96   EXT. ATLANTIC AVENUE- NIGHT

Searching for JANE, HORACE looks across the street...

A PROSTITUTE opens a JOHN'S pants, working on him in a
doorway, the MAN drunk, pinned. There is no spark, no joy.
Pure ugliness.

HORACE looks away, moving down the street.

97   EXT. ALLEYWAY BEHIND BAR- NIGHT

The SWEATING MAN leads JANE down a back alley of filth.
SOUND from the bar is distorted MUSIC, nightmarish VOICES.

98   EXT. BALTIC AVENUE- NIGHT

The low rent street in Monopoly and in real life-- RAPID SHOTS
as HORACE searches for JANE in bars that read like a boozer's
litany: Johnny Gibbons, H & L Lounge, The Saxony, The Trinidad.
HORACE looking into windows of each, no JANE.

99   EXT. ALLEYWAY- NIGHT

A needle falls from JANE'S hand. JANE closing her eyes
in release.

100   EXT. BOARDWALK BENCH AREA- SAME MOMENT

HORACE sits, looking out at ocean BLACKNESS. The SOUND of
Atlantic City-- chatting TOURISTS, arcade BUZZERS and BELLS,
night MUSIC-- fills the air.

101   EXT. ALLEYWAY- SAME

JANE high, not noticing...

The SWEATING MAN rifling her purse for money. None. P.o.ed,
he looks at JANE. Her Camera Girl skirt is hiked up to show
legs.

102   EXT. BOARDWALK BENCHES- SAME

HORACE with deja vu, a feeling of total helplessness-- BUZZERS
AND BELLS, VOICES, MUSIC in his ears.

103   EXT. ALLEYWAY- SAME

JANE'S EYES open. The SWEATING MAN on her. Brutal kisses.

104   EXT. BOARDWALK BENCHES- SAME

HORACE'S EYES close. VOICES and MUSIC out. SILENCE...

105   EXT. ALLEYWAY- SAME

JANE fighting... He pins her... JANE'S tears... SILENCE...

106   EXT. BOARDWALK BENCHES- SAME

HORACE opens eyes. The SOUND of Atlantic City rushing back
at him at once, like an ocean wave, as we:

JUMP CUT TO:
107   INT. H & J'S ROOM- SAME NIGHT/6 A.M.

HORACE turning to see...

JANE, crashed out on the bed beside him. TV LIGHT only.
Still in her dirty Camera Girl outfit, one-arm dangles
from the bed. HORACE pausing a long moment, lifting
her lifeless arm back on the bed, touching her hair
once, twice, her face.

JANE up fast, stoned and startled, with violence,
instinctively punching, fists flailing as with the
SWEATING MAN, HORACE trying to grab hold.

                    HORACE
          Hey! HEY!

JANE only now seeing it's HORACE, stopping. Tears from JANE.
HORACE'S confusion. As we:

FADE TO BLACK & FADE UP ON:
108   EXT. INTERIOR HALLWAY- DAY- DAYS LATER

P.O.V, through the hallway to H & J'S room, the door opening
to find...

LUCINDA. JANE'S friend from the Dumpling House. Surreally
seated at the living room table. No sign of JANE.

>   LUCINDA
>   (icy cool)
>   Hello Horace.

109 INT. H & J'S ROOM- SAME

ANGLE HORACE, entering confused, looking to LUCINDA and the table.

HORACE'S P.O.V, heroin on a mirror. Routine as Sunday dinner.

>   LUCINDA
>   Do you remember me?

HORACE without a word, furiously, to the bathroom. LUCINDA
stoned, amused at his reaction, lighting a cigarette.

>   LUCINDA(O.S.)
>   Lucinda. Jane asked me down. She
>   didn't think you'd mind. Just for
>   a couple days.

ANGLE BATHROOM, HORACE violently splashing water on his face.
Flushing the toilet. Watching it drain.

ANGLE LUCINDA, as HORACE emerges.

>   HORACE
>   Where is she?

>   LUCINDA
>   She went for beer. She'll be back.

HORACE sits, pushing the heroin away.

>   LUCINDA
>   It's not for her. I brought it down.
>   You shouldn't get angry.

>   HORACE
>   I'm not angry.

>   LUCINDA
>   I can tell when a person's angry. They
>   produce an energy. It's counterproductive.

>   HORACE
>   I'm not angry.

A long uncomfortable pause, before:

           HORACE
I heard your best friend killed herself.

           LUCINDA
             (casually)
Oh, yeah.

           HORACE
Jane said you were pretty shaken up.
             (more pause)
What happened?

           LUCINDA
I don't know. Disgusted I guess. We
weren't that close.

           HORACE
I thought she was your best friend.

           LUCINDA
No.

Lies and more fucking lies-- HORACE starts the toy duck, it
moves round and about the heroin.

           HORACE
             (anger in every word)
How's New York?

           LUCINDA
You know New York. It's shit.

           HORACE
Total shit.

           LUCINDA
Total shit. That about covers it.
             (ANOTHER PAUSE)
I just wanted to come down for a couple
days. I didn't mean to cause a problem.

           HORACE
You won't.

           LUCINDA
You see what I brought down? Someone
bought it for me. 60 dollars. Check it
out.

Holding up a two-piece bathing suit against herself, looking
sexy as hell.

                    LUCINDA
          Nice?

HORACE pretending not to notice.

                    LUCINDA
          Why not. Get a little color. Look
          at me. Like a ghost or something.
          Compared to you.

Holding her arm up to HORACE'S, a sexual look flashes
between them, as...

JANE enters, bag in hand, seeing HORACE and LUCINDA, smiling.

DISSOLVE TO:
110 EXT. JOHNNY GIBBONS BAR- LATE NIGHT

Outside another dirt bar, HORACE argues with JANE, LUCINDA
nearby. OVER:

                    HORACE(V.O.)
          I was long since tired of the Baltic
          Avenue bars I found her in. 5 a.m.
          streetscenes. The muggings. Sick-
          nesses.

HORACE and JANE curse each other. JANE walks off with
LUCINDA. HORACE watches them go.

111 INT. CRAPS SCHOOL- DAY

HORACE practices with dice, LAUGHTER behind him, a VOICE:

                    BIANCHI(O.S.)
          -- She don't understand my anger? Wants
          me to forgive myself? Get in touch with
          my feelings?...

CAMERA finds BIANCHI with several STUDENTS, holding court:

                    BIANCHI
          See, my wife doesn't get it. The
          bottle stays on the coffeetable. That
          way the man can rub it when he needs to.
          You get that pink puff of smoke and out
          she comes in those pink pijamas. And she
          says sweetly, so sweetly: 'Yes, Master?'
          Yes, Master.

LOW ANGLE HORACE, staring down at the dice which say it all:
12 craps. Loser. Amidst the LAUGHTER, he walks out of the
room.

112   INT. H & J 'S ROOM- LATER

RAPID SHOTS... HORACE in the room. Day to night. Night
to day. No JANE. HORACE sleepless. Looking awful. OVER:

                    HORACE(V.O.)
          The way it happens. The way it seems to
          be. You choose a life, then it chooses
          you.

113   EXT. UNDER GARDEN PIER- NIGHT/5 A.M.

HORACE looks out. Hellish BLACKNESS. White foam. OVER:

                    HORACE(V.O.)
          I played the fool. Bad weeks found me
          hanging on. Hanging on 'til the Baltic
          Avenue sun came all the way through.

114   INT. H & J'S ROOM- NIGHT

JANE dancing (facing away) in the French Maid's outfit.
HORACE on the bed, loving it. JANE turning fast to show...

CLOSE ON JANE, no makeup this time, no faking it. Real skin
        peeling away... real death. The MUSIC madness, as is
her LAUGHTER.

FLASH TO:
115   EXT. UNDER GARDEN PIER- HORACE

Up fast! On the sand... nightmare!...a nightmare... HORACE
rising, shaking off sand, into bright sunlight like a zombie.
TOURISTS watch him pass with a long look, but HORACE doesn't
see them, moving away.

116   INT. STAIRCASE- THE PRINCETON- DAY/LATER

HORACE dead on his feet, up the narrow stairs.

117   EXT. H & J'S ROOM- SAME

HORACE pushing the door open, not even caring what he finds
this time, surprised though, to see...

118   INT. H & J'S ROOM— SAME

LUCINDA. Watching Saturday cartoons.   <u>No JANE</u>.

HORACE drops into a chair, numb.

> LUCINDA
> I'm bored with this TV.

SILENCE. After a pause:

> LUCINDA
> How is it outside? It's been cold.
> Three days now, I can't get warm.

LUCINDA stretching in a short nightgown, showing flesh.
HORACE meant to notice, and notices.

> HORACE
> Try an extra pair of socks.

> LUCINDA
> (smiling/meaning the nighty)
> I just got this. Do you like it?

> HORACE
> (w/deep fatigue)
> Where's Jane?

Casually, lying:

> LUCINDA
> I don't know.

Knowing she's lying:

> HORACE
> You don't know where she is?

> LUCINDA
> (coldly)
> No.

> HORACE
> But you can tell me where she cops at.

Pause, and:

> LUCINDA
> No. I couldn't do that.

                        HORACE
                      (cracking)
          You <u>FUCKING WILL DO THAT!</u>...
                      (stopping himself)
          Where is she?

                        LUCINDA
                        (icy)
          I don't know.

HORACE disgusted/exhausted, looking away. Another pause:

                        LUCINDA
                      (about her nighty)
          It was given to me as a gift. By an
          admirer.
                      (MORE SILENCE from HORACE)
          I don't see the point in paying for
          something if it's given to you. I
          mean, why pay?

ANGLE ON TELEVISION CARTOONS:

                        LUCINDA(O.S.)
          I believe there's a war going on.

                        HORACE(O.S.)
          How do you mean?

                        LUCINDA(O.S.)
          Men and women. Men want something
          very specific. But women also want
          things. It's like war.

ANGLE HORACE AND LUCINDA:

                        LUCINDA
          There have been times I could have
          killed a man while making love to him.
          I've wanted to but stopped myself. I'd
          use a knife to do it. Or I could use
          my mouth. I'm certain I could do it.
                      (pause)
          Then there are other times I don't
          want to.

HORACE in disbelief, as she goes on:

                        LUCINDA
          Of course there needs to be a greater
          self-discipline. You must be your own
          master...

CONTINUED:

                         LUCINDA(CONT.)
                    (pause)
          Many women don't like me. Even Jane
          sometimes.

                         HORACE
          Maybe she doesn't understand you.

Looking straight at him:

                         LUCINDA
          Do you?

HORACE looks straight back-- Payback? Or something more?-- A
real desperation in HORACE, but seeing a new chance.

                         HORACE
          Yeah. I do.

ANGLE CARTOONS:

                         LUCINDA(O.S.)
          They think I'm a whore. They think I'm
          stealing their men. They're the whores.
          If a woman wanted, she could corrupt
          any man she wanted without a problem.
          Men are so easily corrupted. They have
          no control whatsoever. They only see
          what's in front of them. It affects
          their priorities. Makes them forget
          what they believe in.

                         HORACE
          How do you think Jane feels about us
          being alone together?

                         LUCINDA
          I don't know. You're not married.
          You need an element of freedom in
          any relationship.
                    (smiling)
          I'll tell you about an experience I had.
          It was interesting.

CLOSE ON LUCINDA/HORACE:

                         LUCINDA
          I tried hitchhiking coming down here.
          I'd never done it. I got dressed up
          in something nice like this and went out
          to the highway. I liked it. Some very
          nice men picked me up.

                    HORACE
          You hitchhiked in an outfit like that?

                    LUCINDA
          It didn't take long.

                    HORACE
          No. It wouldn't.
                    (&)
          You should be more careful. That's
          a good way to get raped.

                    LUCINDA
          I know it is.

CLOSE ON HORACE, a look of repulsion.

                    LUCINDA
          What could they have done? Kill me?
          They didn't want to kill me. We had
          an afternoon together. Then they let
          me out.

                    HORACE
          You did it on purpose?

                    LUCINDA
          I suppose it could have been dangerous.
          I really didn't think about it. I mean
          there's danger in anything, if that's
          the way you look at it.

Again a turn, revealing flesh:

                    LUCINDA
          I like being taken. Just the possibility
          of getting caught. Even here with you.

                    HORACE
          Let's go out--

                    LUCINDA
          Right here!

                    HORACE
          She could walk in any minute.

                    LUCINDA
          You're a hypocrite!

                    HORACE
          And you're fucked, lady.

HORACE moving for the door...

                    LUCINDA
          You're weak. No wonder she uses you.
          You lick the whip.

HORACE with disgust, for her, for himself, turning back with
a single look at LUCINDA, slamming the door shut.

119 INT. H & J'S ROOM- MINUTES LATER

A savage FLASH, more like violence than sex, HORACE pinning
LUCINDA, turning her around and ripping off her nighty,
moving together, a BLUR of sexual motion.

120 INT. H & J'S ROOM- MOMENTS LATER

JANE walks in. Ugly. "East Side" JANE on the downside of a 3
day binge. Seeing LUCINDA legs wide, putting a shoe on. HORACE
with a sideways look. JANE seeing it all in a flash. And we
hear SCREAMING...

121 INT. H & J'S ROOM- SECONDS LATER

JANE SCREAMING, a savage blur of motion, at HORACE, flailing
with fists, kicks, knocking over tables, chairs, lamps, the
fight wrecking the place in seconds.

                    HORACE
          TELL ME IT'S OVER! TELL ME IT'S OVER!

JANE picks up a knife, stopping breathless, looking at HORACE.
HORACE equally breathless, coming forward..

                    HORACE
          Say it. Say the words.

Leaning against the knife, pushing his body flush against the
edge...

JANE pauses. Backing off. Dropping the knife.

                    HORACE
          I wanted your attention. Did I get it?
          It was the only way to get her out of
          here!

                    JANE
          You fucked her for me!? You fucked that
          skanky bitch for me!?

LUCINDA silent, cowering in a corner, looking for cover.

                    HORACE
          That's right.

                    JANE
          For me!

                    HORACE
                (w/utter desperation)
          What am I supposed to do!?

JANE repeating the same words, mocking HORACE:

                    HORACE
          You don't come home for weeks. You
          don't eat anymore. What do you do?

                    JANE
          Whatever I please!

                    HORACE
          You look a little piqued. Here...

Moving to her with the toy duck, taking jellybeans from its
bill, trying to feed them to JANE, who shoves him off.

                    JANE
          Fuck you--

                    HORACE
          Have some--

                    JANE
          Fuck you!--

                    HORACE
          Have some...

Reaching for her, forcing her mouth open, shoving jellybeans
inside, one after another...

                    HORACE
          Have some!

Dropping the duck, the jellybeans scatter everywhere. JANE
stoned and collapsed at his feet.

                    HORACE
                (meaning Lucinda)
          Least she's still alive between the legs.

Taking up his jacket, moving for the door...

JANE high, rising in a moment furiously, picking up the knife, coming at him.

LUCINDA SCREAMING.

JANE SCREAMING.

The knife into HORACE.

HORACE looking at his shoulder, the knife stuck there, right through his jacket. HORACE drops. Going down in a heap.

JANE with a look of horror.

OVERHEAD ON ALL, LUCINDA freaked, out the door without a word. JANE, as if only now realizing what she's done, moving to to HORACE...

CLOSE ON JANE AND HORACE, JANE bending to hold him. HORACE in shock, just looking to JANE, blood oozing from him, as we:

DISSOLVE TO:
122 INT. H & J'S ROOM- DAY

HORACE lays in bed with an Ace bandage wrapped around his shoulder. JANE is serving him soup. Their eyes meet. Not a word between them.

DISSOLVE TO:
123 INT. BATHROOM- H & J'S- A DAY LATER

JANE washing the wound at the sink. HORACE turned away.

> JANE
> (falsely, desperately upbeat)
> There. Don't look bad. Kinda gives ya
> character! A couple inches to the skin.
> Doc said no big deal, right? Oh, he gave
> me the pain scrip. I won't swipe it, I
> promise. It's good stuff. Take it from
> an expert!

HORACE silent. JANE splashing water on him.

> JANE
> Lucy musta split. All her stuff's gone.
> Maybe she thinks I killed you.
> (MORE SPLASHING/SILENCE)
> Oh, and I got the meeting at the clinic
> tomorrow. The counselor set it up.
> I told him I wanted to get it together.
> Back the way it was, right...

CONTINUED:

                    JANE(CONT.)
        ...He said you should come down too.
        I mean, if you wanna. It's up to you.
        You wanna go, Hon'? Honey?

HORACE not looking at her. JANE closer, seeing in the mirror
reflection, in his eyes, a <u>finality</u>, stopping.

                    JANE
        Horace?

JANE begins to cry. HORACE looking straight out, expressionless. The SCREEN to FLASHING to WHITE... and HORACE'S VOICE:

                    HORACE(V.O.)
        Somebody, somewhere, once said it:
        Between grief and nothing, I'll take
        grief.

FADE UP ON:
124 EXT. UNDER THE BOARDWALK- MARGATE BEACH- MORNING

HORACE looking out at the ocean, his face expressionless as
before. OVER:

                    HORACE(V.O.)
        I think about that sometimes when people
        ask me why, why did I stay with her?

HORACE gets up, walking. The beach abandoned. Behind him,
Lucy The Elephant. In the distance a sunrise, five-color magic.
OVER:

                    HORACE(V.O.)
        To them I can only say: It seemed like
        the right thing to do. We were in the
        fight of our lives, and we survived.

125 EXT. BOARDWALK- DAY- LATER

HORACE walking, the Boardwalk jammed with TOURISTS. Stopping
in front of a casino. OVER:

                    HORACE(V.O.)
        See, they'll tell you you can't win here.
        The odds are against it, and that's a
        fact. But that's the heart of this place.
        It's like beating death in a way, beating
        what has to be.

126 EXT. BOARDWALK- DAY- MOMENTS LATER

HORACE walking. Stopping again, this time amidst commotion in
front of a tourist shop, Peanutworld. Looking across to see...

ANGLE JANE, standing high on a chair, arms raised, giving a wild
carni-like sales to a crowd of TOURISTS, literally stopping
Boardwalk traffic. OVER:

                    HORACE(V.O.)
          It's what keeps the tourists coming.
          It's what makes winning a hopeless bet
          so sweet. Beating the odds. It happens.
          Down here, it happens all the time.

CLOSE ON HORACE, just smiling, waving to her.

CLOSE ON JANE, seeing HORACE and waving back wildly.

MUSIC UP, a wild Tito Puente SALSA, and...

128 EXT. ROLLERCOASTER- STEEL PIER- DAY- LATER

CAMERA REVERSED on HORACE and JANE, flying at top speed on the
rollercoaster, both SCREAMING.

129 EXT. WATER PISTOL ARCADE- STEEL PIER- LATER

HORACE and JANE firing into the mouths of clowns, JANE popping
a balloon before HORACE, winning the game, jumping for joy,
rubbing it in HORACE'S face with kisses.

130 EXT. OCEAN 1 PIER- NIGHT

HORACE and JANE decked out in their Saturday night best,
Dancing on the deck on a huge pier shaped like an ocean
liner. The whole of Atlantic City lit up like streaks
of pearls below them. Turning toward the CAMERA, and...

MATCH CUT TO:
131 INT. MEXICAN RESTAURANT- NIGHT- LATER

Turning toward CAMERA on a miniature dancefloor, doing the
tango...She, with sombrero and rose in mouth; He, cheek to
cheek, spinning her back 'n forth, bee line, spinning again.

A WAITER approaches a table and leaves off a pitcher of
margaritas and two glasses.

HORACE and JANE spin off, moving for the drinks.

                    HORACE
          Baby! Your first day!

                    JANE
          Honey, what can I say!

                    HORACE
          Peanutworld! The world of peanuts!

                    JANE
          It's more than peanuts, you dodo! You
          saw me talking up those sunglasses! You
          saw the style, the savoir-faire!

The WAITER returns.

                    HORACE
          Just a plate of nachos for now.

The WAITER about to go...

                    JANE
          Tell the chef to put extra cheese on 'em!
          We haven't eaten in six or seven days.

The WAITER unamused, forcing a smile, leaves.

                    JANE
          Look what else! Look at these.
                    (EMPTIES FULL CONTENTS OF BAG)
          Flashy, right!?
                    (MODELS .99 CENT EARRINGS)
          Or these?
                    (MODELS SNOW CONE EARRINGS)
          A little more casual, for when I work the
          ice cream stand. Hey, Bub!

HORACE filling his glass with booze.

                    JANE
          That's your third, I'm on my first!
          Don't hog it!
                    (PICKING UP HER KNIFE)
          I can get tough if I have to!

A pause a moment, both of them laughing, JANE shrinking up
with a coy smile:

                    JANE
          Ooops.

HORACE all smiles. Filling her glass. Toasting:

                    HORACE
          Here's to Peanutworld!

                    JANE
          Big bucks, honey!

They toast and drink.

                    HORACE
          But listen, I don't want you bringing home
          any junk, ok? No refrigerator magnets,
          no frog families, Indonesian coconutheads--

                    JANE
          They got some nice pieces in there!

                    HORACE
          Gimme a break!

                    JANE
          You should see the brass they have!
          Remember my father's brass collection?
          I gotta pick up a few pieces for him!
          They got brass dice too, Hon'. I'm
          gonna get you a pair of brass dice!

The WAITER returns with nachos.

                    WAITER
          Here you go.

He turns to leave. JANE glancing at the dish...

                    JANE
          Ah, excuse me, por favor!

                    HORACE
          What's wrong?

                    JANE
          Honey, look at that plate. There's
          no cheese. They're supposed to be
          covered in cheese. Look...

CONTINUED:

> JANE(CONT.)
> (HOLDS UP A CHIP)
> Poor old taco.

> HORACE
> That's a tortilla chip.

> JANE
> Poor old chip. He's naked.

> HORACE
> I'll take it back.

The WAITER takes the plate away. As she goes:

> JANE
> Thank you! Oh, and bring some adhesive
> tape! You don't know the way he drinks!
> (to HORACE)
> Nice guy.

> HORACE
> I had a feeling I was gonna be embarrassed
> tonight.

> JANE
> I hadda do it. You saw 'em.

> HORACE
> You have a way about you. That certain
> something.

> JANE
> That's the kinda hairpin I am! Honey,
> they broke the mold when they put this
> piece together, believe it!
> (&)
> Thanks for coming down today.

> HORACE
> You were on a hellava roll.

> JANE
> You saw me! Drawing 'em in from all over
> the Boardwalk! My manager said I was a
> natural born salesgirl. He's gonna let
> me work the sunglasses stand now 'til
> when the tourists go in September. At
> .50 cents commission on every pair I
> sell, that's big bucks, honey!...

CONTINUED:

                   JANE(CONT.)
...I'm gonna buy myself some nice things
for once! Clothes. Accessories and whatnot.

                   HORACE
Gonna be nice having money in your pocket.

                   JANE
My own money!

                   HORACE
Your own money.

                   JANE
My Daddy won't ever have to do for me
again!

                   HORACE
He won't believe it.

Realizing, and the thought almost brings tears:

                   JANE
I really did it, didn't I?

Realizing the importance of this for her, this simple thing
a real triumph:

                   HORACE
You really did.

They kiss long and lovingly. The bored WAITER returns with
nachos.

                   WAITER
This should be better.

                   HORACE
It's fine.

JANE looks to the plate. HORACE and the WAITER look to JANE
for the verdict. She picks up a chip, and frowns.

                   HORACE
Jane--

                   JANE
                   (points)
Yeah, well...Honey, see the edges.
They're uncovered. The whole outside
edge is uncovered.

                    WAITER
          I'll bring it back.

                    JANE
          No, no! I feel bad...

Rising, plate in hand:

                    JANE
          Let me go back and talk with the chef--

                    HORACE
          Jane--

                    WAITER
          You don't have to do that.

The WAITER tries to take the plate back but JANE is on a roll.

                    JANE
          Don't worry, Honey! I've waitressed
          before. I can't send you back to him
          alone. I'm sure he's a nice man--

                    HORACE
          Jane!

                    JANE
          I'll be right back, Jimmy! Or was it
          Billy? Oh, these men get me so confused!

Walking off with the WAITER:

                    JANE
          I just love the place though. There's
          one like it in New York in the Village.
          On the West Side!

HORACE is laughing at the table, as...

ANGLE DOORS, from the kitchen emerges the CHEF himself. His
large figure filling the FRAME with the white of his smock,
CAMERA BOOMS up and behind him as JANE walks, plate in hand
and Hollywood smile, right at the CHEF and us, into FULL
FRAME...

                    JANE
                 (to the CHEF)
          Oh hello, my good man!

CUT TO:
131 EXT. ATLANTIC CITY BUS TERMINAL- DAY

HORACE and JANE kiss goodbye among TRAVELLERS.   JANE jumps
on board.   OVER:

>   HORACE(V.O.)
>   Saturday afternoon at the Atlantic City
>   bus station.   Jane was taking a four day
>   trip to New York.   She was missing her
>   father and fearing for him the closer
>   he got to California.

ANGLE HORACE, JANE'S face in a window as the bus moves out.
OVER:

>   HORACE(V.O.)
>   We made promises to be better to each
>   other.   A kiss and she was gone.

HORACE turning to CAMERA...

MATCH CUT TO:
132   INT. INTENSIVE CARE UNIT- HOSPITAL- DAYS LATER

HORACE turning to CAMERA... he is sitting in a chair.   His face
now masked and his eyes, devastated.   OVER:

>   HORACE(V.O.)
>   I called her father's place about a
>   week later.   She was gone.   The two
>   of them had argued.   I don't know
>   what happened.   About a week later
>   I got a call saying they found her.

CLOSE UP ON JANE'S FACE, this a hideous picture, for she is
unrecognizable, unconscious and bloated under white hospital
linen, sucking through a respirator tube.   The SOUND of
respirated AIR, and the whiteness of the room dazzling.
OVER:

>   HORACE(V.O.)
>   They didn't even know who she was at
>   first.   Jane Doe.

A masked NURSE comes into the room, passing HORACE, picking up
JANE'S chart, reading.   Passing HORACE on her way out.   OVER:

>   HORACE(V.O.)
>   What was worse was that they didn't know
>   what was wrong with her.   Poisoned smack.
>   Overdose.   They busied themselves taking
>   blood tests.   Her lungs were shot from
>   the reaction.   Her kidney's pouring
>   liquids through her body.   She had blown
>   up like a party balloon.   Critical.

HORACE rising as the NURSE goes. Moving to JANE. OVER:

                    HORACE(V.O.)
          The next day I went to see Jane.

JANE stirs, semi-conscious. HORACE closer. Her eyes
meeting his. Looking away. OVER:

                    HORACE(V.O.)
          It was a mistake.

133 INT. BUS- LINCOLN TUNNEL- NIGHT

PAN empty seats. CAMERA finds HORACE. Weeping. And tunnel
light.

134 EXT. PHONE BOOTH- BOARDWALK- NEXT DAY

HORACE in a dealer's outfit at a pay telephone, dialing. OVER:

                    HORACE(V.O)
          I got back on the bus the same afternoon.
          I had to work. The next day I got another
          call I never asked for.

The phone connection poor...

                    HORACE
          --Someone died. A message on 312. I don't
          know who. I'm sorry? I can't hear you.
          Room 312.

                    VOICE
                  (emotionless)
          Jane Marie Gerasi? She died last
          night. Are you family? Hello?
          Hello?

A single GULL SQUAWKS from a roof. Launching off. The
SOUND OUT. SILENCE in flight...

DISSOLVE&SUPERIMPOSE:
135 INT. INTENSIVE CARE UNIT- THE NIGHT BEFORE

JANE'S FACE, no breath. The respirator SOUND has died.

SILENCE...

CUT TO:
136 EXT. PHONE BOOTH- BOARDWALK- DAY- A MOMENT LATER

TOURISTS pass. The booth empty. The phone dangles.
The PICTURE DISSOLVING into WHITE...

The SOUND of WATER SPLASHING. And JANE'S VOICE:

>   JANE(V.O.)
>   Well I'm just lying here in the tub now.
>   Horace and I have had a wonderful night
>   together. We're planning on doing some-
>   thing tomorrow. I don't know...
>   (SPLASHING WATER/LAUGHTER)
>   I don't know what else...Stop!
>   (SPLASHING WATER/LAUGHTER)
>   I don't know what else to say! Stop it!
>   STOP!

FADE UP ON:
137 INT. H & J'S ROOM- DAY

HORACE turns off the tape recorder. Pausing a moment.

OVERHEAD TO SHOW THE ROOM, empty... walls, tables, closets
packed up, the menagerie of Jane's world stripped bare,
her possessions packed into garbage bags at HORACE'S
feet. HORACE stuffing the recorder into the last open
bag, tying it off. OVER:

>   HORACE(V.O.)
>   I rode in the funeral car with a distant
>   aunt of hers. She told me stories about
>   Jane twenty years before. She was a girl
>   of eight again, with long brown curls
>   her aunt used to arrange in yellow bows
>   and ribbons. Her mother had died. Jane
>   begged her aunt to be her mother. But
>   it didn't work out that way.

138 EXT. PRINCETON ANTIQUES/ROOMINGHOUSE- DAY

HORACE packing bags into the trunk of a waiting cab. OVER:

>   HORACE(V.O.)
>   I left her father on his last day in
>   Bayonne. He was feeding birds in the
>   yard. Scattering seed and warding off
>   his six enormous dogs when they chased
>   after them. There was some commotion
>   and he loved it.

139 EXT. SALVATION ARMY- DAY

HORACE at a red Salvation Army dumpster, jamming in a bag of
JANE'S possessions, and another, another. Something falls out
of the last bag. OVER:

> HORACE(V.O.)
> I remember the way he talked about busting
> up bars in the '30s. The craps games.
> And her smile. That movie star smile she
> flashed.

HORACE picks up the pink toy duck. Numb, walking off. OVER:

> HORACE(V.O.)
> I remember the way he talked like a
> possessed man. An empty man who just
> discovered his life meant nothing.

140 EXT. BOARDWALK- DAY

HORACE walks toward us (as in the beginning of the FILM).
All of Atlantic City is behind him. OVER:

> HORACE(V.O.)
> I hated to leave him that afternoon.
> I remember his face at the door. And
> the door closing. I remember it all.

141 EXT. HIGHWAY MEDIAN- DAY- A MOMENT LATER

HORACE stuck in the center of the four lane highway. Cradling
the duck as cars pass and HORNS blast, he sets it down and
turns it on...

CLOSE ON THE DUCK, it turns and shakes, flapping wings, whirling
as if with a life of its own.

CLOSE ON HORACE, watching the duck, cracking a smile. OVER:

> HORACE(V.O.)
> I have no choice.

FLASH SHOTS OF JANE... Dancing with the duck. The food
fight with HORACE. Lovemaking. Laughing in "death" makeup.
Kissing him under the Boardwalk. Walking in sunset. Selling
tourists at Peanutworld. Dancing...

BACK TO HORACE, in the middle of noon day traffic, beginning
to dance the duck dance, flapping his arms like the bird and
JANE, laughing.

MUSIC merges with the dance.   HORACE spinning, spinning,
the SCREEN FLASHING to WHITE.

FADE IN A TITLE:

                    FOR   CLAIRE

                    FIN.

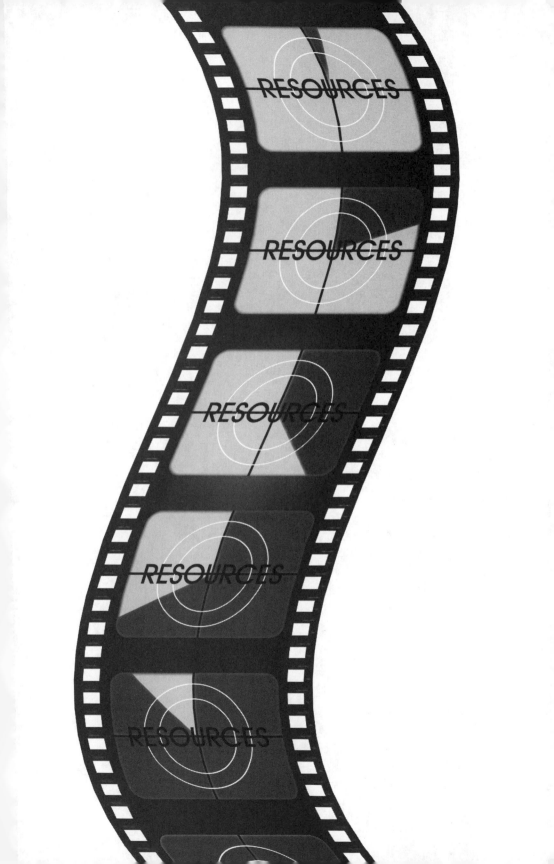

Resources

Essential Resources

- Canadian Intellectual Property Office
  www.cipo.ic.gc.ca

- Internet Movie Database
  www.imdb.com

- U.S. Copyright Office
  www.copyright.gov

- Writers Guild of America East
  www.wgaeast.org

- Writers Guild of America West
  www.wga.org

- Writers Guild of Canada
  www.wgc.ca

Must-Read Screenwriting Books

- *The 21st Century Screenplay*
  by Linda Aronson

- *Hollywood Representation Directory*

- *How to Write a Movie in 21 Days*
  by Viki King

- *Screenplay: The Foundations of Screenwriting*
  by Syd Field

- *The Screenwriter's Bible: A Complete Guide to Writing, Formatting, and Selling Your Script*
  by David Trottier

- *Writing Screenplays that Sell*
  by Michael Hauge

- *Save the Cat!* book series
  by Blake Snyder

Screenwriting Magazines

- *Fade In Magazine*
  www.fadeinmag.com

- *Filmmaker Magazine*
  www.filmmakermagazine.com

- *Hollywood Scriptwriter*
  www.hollywoodscriptwriter.com

- *Canadian Screenwriter Magazine*
  www.writersguildofcanada.com/magazine

- *Script Magazine*
  www.scriptmag.com/category/magazine

- *The Hollywood Reporter*
  www.hollywoodreporter.com

- *Variety*
  www.variety.com

- *Writer's Digest*
  www.writersdigest.com

- *Written By* (magazine by Writers Guild of America)
  www.wga.org/writtenby/writtenby.aspx

Screenwriting Forums

- Amazon Studios
  http://studios.amazon.com

- Done Deal Professional
  www.donedealpro.com

- Drew's Script-O-Rama
  www.script-o-rama.com

- Inktip
  www.inktip.com

- Movie Bytes
  www.moviebytes.com

- MovieMaker
  www.moviemaker.com

- Script Shadow
  www.scriptshadow.blogspot.com

- Simply Scripts
  www.simplyscripts.com

- Story Notes from Hell
  http://storynotesfromhell.com

- Syd Field's Screenwriting
  www.sydfield.com

- Talentville
  www.talentville.com

- Trigger Street Labs
  www.triggerstreet.com

- Wordplay
  www.wordplayer.com

Well-Known Screenwriting Schools (in Canada and the United States)

- American Film Institute Conservatory (Los Angeles, CA)
  www.afi.com/conservatory/about/screenwriting.aspx

- Boston University (Boston, MA)
  www.bu.edu/com/academics/film-tv/graduate

- Chapman University (Orange, CA)
  www.ftv.chapman.edu/programs/
  conservatory_of_motion_pictures/mfa_screenwriting

- Columbia College (Chicago, IL)
  www.colum.edu/academics/film_and_video/
  Undergraduate_Program/Screenwriting.php

- Columbia University (New York, NY)
  www.arts.columbia.edu/film

- Loyola Marymount College (Los Angeles, CA)
  http://sftv.lmu.edu/programs/screenwriting.htm

- Mediabistro (online)
  www.mediabistro.com/courses

- The New School (New York, NY)
  www.newschool.edu/media-studies

- New York Film Academy (New York, NY)
  www.nyfa.edu

- New York University: Tisch School Of The Arts
  (New York, NY)
  www.specialprograms.tisch.nyu.edu/object/
  screenwritingcert.html

- Toronto Film School (Toronto, ON)
  www.torontofilmschool.ca/screenwriting.asp

- University of California (Los Angeles, CA)
  www.tft.ucla.edu/programs/screenwriting

- University of Miami (Miami, MI)
  www.com.miami.edu/mfamotionpictures

- University of Southern California (Los Angeles, CA)
  http://cinema.usc.edu/writing/index.cfm

- University of Texas (Austin, TX)
  http://rtf.utexas.edu

- Vancouver Film School (Vancouver, BC)
  www.vfs.com/programs/writing

- York University (Toronto, ON)
  www.yorku.ca/gradfilm/mfas/index.html

Screenwriting Blogs

- The Artful Writer
  www.artfulwriter.com
  Craig Mazin's personal website. Though he no longer updates
  it, the website has more than four years' of information for
  new screenwriters. He now hosts a podcast with John August
  and the podcast can be found at www.johnaugust.com/podcast

- Bachelors Degree
  www.bachelorsdegree.org/2010/10/12/
  60-best-blogs-for-aspiring-screenwriters
  This link offers new screenwriters a list of the 60 best blogs
  for them to follow.

- The Black List
  www.deadline.com/2011/12/
  the-black-list-2011-screenplay-roster
  www.deadline.com/2010/12/the-black-list-2010
  This list is complied of the best scripts written by unknown
  screenwriters in that given year. The list is not a "best of"
  list but rather a "most liked" list created from suggestions
  made by various film executives. Some notable graduates of
  the Black List are *Juno* and *500 Days of Summer*.

- Go Into The Story
  www.gointothestory.com
  Scott Myers is a screenwriter and instructor at UCLA Ex-
  tension Writers' Program. His blog was created to give his
  students (and other aspiring screenwriters) a platform to
  discuss the creative process of screenwriting.

- ItsontheGrid
  www.itsonthegrid.com
  This website is a database that catalogues information about
  feature films in Hollywood dating back 25 years. You can
  look up any film and find out the names of the production
  company, the management company and studio involved as
  well as managers, producers, directors and writers.

- John August's personal website
  www.johnaugust.com
  August is a screenwriter who uses his website to answer
  reader-submitted questions to help new screenwriters understand how the industry works. He also hosts a podcast
  called "Scriptnotes" with Craig Mazin (also a screenwriter)
  that answers questions about the screenwriting industry.

- Just Effing (Julie Gray's website)
  www.justeffing.com
  Gray is an industry professional who works with large production companies, teaches screenwriting courses, and runs the
  annual Just Effing Entertain Me Screenwriting Competition.
  The site offers information about self-publishing, where her
  next workshops will be, and her script consultant services.

- Script Gods Must Die
  www.scriptgodsmustdie.com
  Coauthor Paul Peditto's website details the scriptwriting

services he offers and provides information about the screen-writing industry based on his own personal experience.

- Script Secrets
www.scriptsecrets.net
William C. Martell is a screenwriter who writes daily screen-writing tips. These tips sometimes discuss particular elements in a script or may break down a new movie's script and explain what worked in it and what didn't. Martell also has a personal website: www.sex-in-a-sub.blogspot.com

- A TV-Calling
www.tv-calling.com
This blog is a source for analysis and information about writing for television. It has many posts on spec script writing, story arcs and character psychology.

- Xtranormal
www.xtranormal.com
This unique website allows users to make short animated films using its software. There are many actors and sets to choose from. The user decides on the story and the script.

Fun Links: Movies That Are Based on True Stories

- Wikipedia: Films Based on Actual Events
www.en.wikipedia.org/wiki/
List_of_films_based_on_actual_events

- Cracked: Movies Based on True Stories That Aren't
www.cracked.com/article_16478_7-movies-based-true-story-that-are-complete-bullshit.html

- Hubpages: 10 Best Movies Based on a True Story
www.kpfingaz.hubpages.com/hub/
10-Best-Movies-Based-On-A-True-Story